6 4977

THE CHANGING STRUCTURE OF THE WESTERN ECONOMY

BEATTY MEMORIAL LECTURES

Published Series

EAST AND WEST

by

RADHAKRISHNAN

1954

THE INTERPLAY OF EAST AND WEST

by

BARBARA WARD

1955

WHITE MEN CAME TO
THE ST. LAWRENCE

by

MORRIS BISHOP

1959

THE PRESENT-DAY EXPERIMENT
IN WESTERN CIVILIZATION

by

ARNOLD TOYNBEE

1961

SIR DOUGLAS COPLAND

THE CHANGING STRUCTURE
OF
THE WESTERN ECONOMY

Beatty Memorial Lectures

McGILL UNIVERSITY PRESS
MONTREAL
1963

PRINTED IN GREAT BRITAIN
in 11 point Baskerville
BY LATIMER, TREND AND CO. LTD.
PLYMOUTH

PREFACE

THE Beatty Lectures, in their published form, have usually served the Montreal audience as an *aide-mémoire* to recall in precise pattern the points that the lecturer made when they listened to him.

In this case, however, the ideas set forth in the following pages will come with as much novelty to the Montreal audience as to the friends of McGill University in distant places and to all those who are interested in the ideas of Sir Douglas Copland. To our deep regret, a serious illness necessitated his admission to hospital on the day after his first lecture, so that the second and third were never delivered. We can read now the thesis that we were not able to hear directly from him, and it is presented to the reader in the happy knowledge that, during the intervening period, Sir Douglas has fully recovered his health and regained the vitality that all his many friends have long admired.

McGill University is indebted to him for the careful preparation of the manuscript and I think that Sir Edward Beatty, outstanding Chancellor who served McGill from 1920 until his death in 1943, would have been deeply interested in this contribution to the series of lectures in which his memory is annually kept before us. No Canadian was more interested than he in

'The Changing Structure of the Western Economy' and its impact upon the development of Canada.

F. CYRIL JAMES
Principal and Vice-Chancellor
McGill University

CONTENTS

INTRODUCTION

I WAS deeply honoured to be invited to deliver the Beatty Lectures at McGill University at the end of 1961. This invitation came after many pleasant associations with McGill, including the award of an honorary degree.

The theme of the Lectures was a basic problem which has interested me for many years, namely, the developing structure of the Western economy and the relationship between the public and private sectors. This has been of particular interest in Australia and New Zealand, the two young countries with which I am most familiar. The whole of the Western economy, however, is experiencing a constructive development in what might be called the establishment of a mixed economy, with varying degrees of the proportion of resources being developed in the public and private sectors. This is a healthy development in that it is based upon the experience and judgement of leaders in public and private enterprise in the several countries, and is not the product of what might be a blind devotion to an ideology.

After delivering the first lecture, I was unfortunately taken ill and had to go to hospital. The remaining two lectures were cancelled and I was denied the opportunity of having seminars that had been arranged for the week following the delivery of the lectures. I had been looking forward very much to these seminars because they would have given me the opportunity of discussing major issues with groups who were familiar with the development of the structure of the Canadian and the United States' economies.

Reference is made in the lectures to a paper I was privileged to present at the conference associated with the Harvard Tercentenary Celebration in 1936. This paper, under the title of 'The State and the Entrepreneur', deals with the developing structure of the free economies. Though prepared over a quarter of a century ago, it seemed to have still a direct application to current problems. I wish to express my thanks to the Harvard University Press for permission to have this paper reprinted in this volume of lectures, and also to McGill University for agreeing to include the paper with the lectures.

DOUGLAS COPLAND

30 April 1962

I

THE MIXED ECONOMY OF THE WEST AND ITS DEVELOPMENT

To the economist attempting to interpret economic trends and outline basic policy in public or private enterprise or in the economy as a whole, the world presents a much more complex picture today than it did less than a quarter of a century ago. This complexity is due to a greatly accelerated rate of change in all phases of human activity in all parts of the modern world. The point was emphasized about twenty-five years ago, with great precision, by the distinguished philosopher, Alfred North Whitehead, appropriately enough in an address at the Harvard Graduate School of Business Administration. After a distinguished academic career in London and Cambridge, he became, at an advanced age, Professor of Philosophy at Harvard. There, in his seventies, he published a book of essays under the challenging title, *Adventures of Ideas*. This was in the dismal thirties, when the Western world was recovering from its greatest depression and was soon to enter upon its most costly and widespread war. After informing his readers that a great society was one in

I

which its men of business thought highly of their functions, Whitehead went on to outline his theme of change in the world to come. He drew attention to the fact that the time-span of life was lengthening. This, of course, was due to one of the great achievements of science, the conquest of lethal disease—or, as it might be named, 'death control'. What was clear to Whitehead twenty-five years ago is only just becoming generally apparent today, though plans to meet the population bulge are still far behind the event in all countries. The counterpart of this lengthening of the time-span of life was, according to Whitehead, the shortening of the time-span of change, owing to the great and spectacular contributions of science and technology to man's conquest and utilization of resources.

These two fundamental changes meet together in promoting a rate of growth far beyond anything the human race has experienced in its long and chequered career on the earth. The lengthening of the time-span of life and the shortening of the time-span of change created the most vital challenge to man in his private capacity, but even more so to him as a member of an organized society. How was this to be met? According to Whitehead, the question turned on what was happening to the time-span of ideas. Was this capable of being adjusted for the individual and, more importantly, for organized society, to meet the new and bewildering situation caused by man's growing conquest of nature and disease?

This is still the unresolved question confronting all individuals and all societies, with their new hopes and aspirations, in all parts of the world. To the economist, it presents perhaps a greater challenge than to the scientist, because the economist is dealing with the impact of rapid technological change on the organization of the economy, and with its political and social ramifications. Never before was the judgement of broad social issues so important for the economist as it is today. It is not enough to be an expert technician. One may doubt whether the jargon and the equations of modern theoretical analysis in economics have provided the economist with the real tools of the trade for the fulfilment of his new responsibilities. Perhaps it would be better if more attention were paid to Alfred Marshall's advice, namely, to use mathematical analysis as the means of elucidating or solving a given economic problem, but then to cast the equations aside and state the wider implications of the problem and its solution in lucid and logical terms. Technical proficiency in theoretical analysis of the economics of a changing world may well prove to be sacrificing the end to the means.

I am reminded of the reaction of the old parson in Christopher Fry's *The Lady's not for Burning*, when he was beset by heresy all around him. Rising apparently bewildered from his chair, he exclaimed that it was all Greek to him, but the trouble was that he understood Greek! I can't assume such eminence, but in these Beatty Lectures for 1961, which I am honoured by McGill to be invited to deliver, I shall endeavour to show why the economist of today, seeking to interpret the economic impact of the new and challenging social technological forces at play in the world, should also be able to say that he 'understands Greek'!

The Impact of the Accelerating Rate of Change

The theme for our consideration is the impact of a rapidly changing world on the structure of the Western economy. It would be strange indeed if the economy of the West were impervious to the new forces that have arisen over the last few decades. It is not merely that these forces have operated in the terrain in which the so-called free economy has developed since the Industrial Revolution. It was then the major economy and, through trade and colonial power, dominated the economies of what might be called the underdeveloped countries. There was nothing to challenge it until the development of the communist structure of modern Russia some forty years ago and, more recently, the liquidation of colonial empires, which has been accompanied by the rising aspirations of the underdeveloped countries to modernize their ancient economic structures.

Thus, in addition to technological developments and the accelerating pace of change, the modern world economy, like Gaul of old, is divided into three parts. This is bound to have an impact upon the shape of things to come in the Western economy; no part of the world today can live in a vacuum. The forces of change thus press from without as well as from within; in both the communist world, now comprising over one-third of the world population, and in the underdeveloped world, with its vast areas and massive and growing population, developments will ensue that are bound to have an impact upon the Western economy and on its plans to meet the new situation confronting it.

Under the impact of new political and social ideas, quite important changes were already taking place in the structure of the Western economy before the communist or underdeveloped economies began to affect the position. They are bound to have an increasing influence in the years immediately ahead, particularly on the rate of growth; on the pattern of investment and development as between the public and private sectors of the Western economy; on the conscious allocation of resources to the provision of power, fuel, and transport, and on the conservation of water as a vital resource; on the development of education and scientific research; and finally, on the encouragement of the arts and the raising of cultural standards. More and more it will be necessary in our economy of free enterprise to plan an allocation of resources towards a desired and considered end. The play of the market cannot be regarded—and has not been so regarded for many years now—as necessarily producing the most desirable economic and social framework in which to develop an economy in order to yield the best fruits of efficiency in an increasingly technical age, or to meet the hopes and aspirations of people for social betterment.

The Importance of the Public Sector

The Western economy is correctly styled a *mixed* economy, with the public sector becoming increasingly important. This new development may most appropriately be measured by considering the proportion of public to private investment; however, a comparison of total expenditure on current social obligations as well as on development—by all public authorities—as a percentage of gross product, would emphasize still more the growing significance of the public sector. In Australia, total investment is approximately one-third public and two-thirds private. This stands perhaps midway between the economies of Canada and the United States, where public investment, though increasing, is still only about one-fifth of total investment, and the economies of advanced social democracies in Europe such as Sweden and the United Kingdom, where the public sector has increased in recent years to between forty and fifty per cent of total investment. The factors determining the relative importance of the public and private sectors, as measured by investment, are partly economic and partly the prevailing social philosophy.

In the case of Australia, both economic and social considerations played an important part in setting the pattern of development; economic considerations perhaps predominated, owing to the importance of water conservation, provision of power and fuel, and transport development on a continent with a small but rapidly-growing population. The public sector in Australia, in fact, provides the framework in which private enterprise makes its distinctive contribution to development. It may be of interest to recall that it was in Australia, in the State of Victoria, that what is known as the statutory authority was first developed. This was the establishment by the Victorian Government, prior to federation, of the State Rivers and Water Supply

Commission, to conserve the waters of the Murray River for irrigation. The Commission is a semi-independent authority, deriving its function and power from an Act of Parliament, but operating in the management and development of the enterprise much as a board of directors exercises its administrative responsibility in a private company. It thus combines, or is capable of combining, some of the principal constructive elements of public and private enterprise.

Since then, many similar authorities have been established by the federal and state governments of Australia, perhaps the most outstanding being the Snowy Mountains Authority, set up by the Commonwealth Government after the war to combine irrigation and the provision of electric power by harnessing the waters of the Snowy River. This is, at the moment, one of the great engineering feats of the Western world. Subject to the provision of finance, the Authority proceeds with its planned programme of development, slightly ahead of schedule and without government intervention in its administration. There are examples of such authorities in Canada and the United States, such as the Canadian National Railways and the Tennessee Valley Authority, but this form of enterprise has been more fully developed in Australia, owing largely to our special conditions requiring concerted public and private enterprise in some major economic projects. It should not be assumed, however, that the relatively high expenditure on public works involves a corresponding increase in the public debt. In the period from 1953–54 to 1960–61, total expenditure by public authorities on public works amounted to £3,827 million, but the increase in the debt of public authorities was only £597 million. The balance, approximately eighty-five per cent, was met from revenue, mainly taxation.

Thus, fiscal policy has been a potent force in diverting current income to public investment in special projects, such as power and fuel, transport, irrigation and communications, as well as assisting in the more accepted forms of government provision for schools and hospitals. It may be argued that this imposes too much responsibility on the present generation in building for the next generation, without some return on that part of its tax burden that is devoted to investment, that is, to building for the future. But if this is an accepted procedure from generation to generation, and in the interests of vigorous and sound economic development, the net cost and return are equitably shared. This point is important in view of the shape of things to come in the vast underdeveloped regions; now embarking upon the reconstruction of their economies and preparing to meet great increases in their populations, they seek to provide better facilities for education and technical training, more opportunities for employment. The economy of the underdeveloped world will become even more mixed in the aggregate than that of the West, with a greater emphasis upon the public sector. Moreover, in the transition, increasing economic aid from the advanced economies to the less-developed ones will be essential, and in the ultimate economic interest of both. This will itself emphasize the importance of concerted action being taken by the advanced countries, and thus in turn bring into greater prominence in such societies public policies on the allocation of resources.

The Challenge of Growth

It is part of the folklore of private enterprise that the less the government spends on, or participates in, the overall direction of economic policy, the sounder and more vigorous will be both the economy as a whole and its rate of growth. This is perhaps the central issue facing the Western economy in the years immediately ahead.

Two basic problems present themselves as an inescapable challenge. The first is the great increase in populations now under way and in prospect for the next three or four decades. The world has some 3,000 million people at the moment but, on all the evidence available, it will about double that number by the end of the century. This would involve an annual increase of 1·5 per cent to 1·75 per cent, but even if the rate were conservatively set at 1·25 per cent—the minimum possible with the prevailing health standards—the population of the world would double in less than sixty years. This is a rate of growth far in excess of anything experienced in history. It comes at a time when there is increasing pressure to raise educational, technical, and living standards. The Western economy will have not only to meet the impact of its own increasing numbers, but also to assist the underdeveloped countries in dealing with their own far less tractable problems of perhaps even greater increasing numbers.

This brings into focus the second basic problem confronting the Western economy, namely, the rate of economic growth appropriate to meet the situation, and how to attain it. The adventure of growth is the challenge before all countries in the world today, and is perhaps even more urgent for the West than for other areas because of its international obligations. The following table taken from the *World Economic Survey 1960* (p. 16), published by the United Nations, gives the rates of growth in real gross domestic product and capital formation as a percentage of gross product, for leading countries in the Western economy for the period 1950–59:

	Annual rate of growth in real domestic product (percentage per year)	Gross capital formation— percentage of gross domestic product
Japan	9·1	28·5
Germany	7·5	23·9
Austria	5·7	21·8
Italy	5·7	20·8
Netherlands	4·6	24·3
Australia	4·3	28·4
Finland	4·2	25·6
France	4·0	18·6
Canada	3·9	24·5
Norway	3·4	29·7
United States	3·3	18·0
Sweden	3·3	21·1
New Zealand	3·1	23·2
Belgium	2·7	16·3
Denmark	2·7	18·9
United Kingdom	2·5	15·6

The differences in the rate of growth are striking, with Japan at 9·1 per cent per annum in the period 1950 to 1959, and the United Kingdom at 2·5 per cent. Australia stands about halfway at 4·6 per cent, and the United States has only 3·3 per cent. Precise figures are not available in the United Nations *World Survey* concerning the rate of growth in the Soviet Union or other communist countries, but in the major basic industries, perhaps with the exception of agriculture, it is well known that Russia has a very high planned rate of growth. Thus, whether it be on account of the internal rate of population growth, the impact of technological change, the rate of growth, present and prospective, in the communist economy, or the new association that must be built with the underdeveloped countries, it will be essential for the Western economy to develop and sustain a higher overall rate of growth than has been customary over the years. This will inevitably involve a greater element of conscious planning and some basic structural changes in the so-called free economy of the West. Whitehead's consideration of the time-span of ideas is the key to the answer to this basic problem, and it will be further examined in the second lecture.

The State and the Entrepreneur

In 1936 I was privileged to be a guest of Harvard University at its Tercentenary and to read a paper on 'The State and the Entrepreneur', published in 1937 in *Authority and the Individual* (Harvard University Press) and included in the Appendix of the present volume. An excerpt follows:

Let me summarize my thesis. The function of the entrepreneur must continue to be performed in any community that desires to make progress. The qualities of imagination, leadership, and adventure necessary for great constructive work were exercised by the entrepreneur under free capitalism. During a large part of the nineteenth century he was left free in most countries to pursue his objective of maximum profit without serious interference by the state. This was true especially of the United States, where even in the post-war period (1919–1929) capitalism flourished and its virtues were extolled as never before in the history of man. Then came the great depression to expose the grave defects of an economic order that had no solution for economic fluctuations and no means of ameliorating the burdens of depression. Capitalism under the control of the entrepreneur guided mainly by considerations of maximum profit is now completely discredited. It does not give economic security to the masses of the people; it does not provide the administrative machinery whereby increased technical efficiency is transformed easily into a generally higher standard of living; it does not furnish society with the social institutions required to meet the strains imposed by economic fluctuations and rapid technical progress; it does not provide the increasing range of free or collective goods that enter more and more into the standard of living. Countries have been able to absorb the shocks of depression and improved technique in inverse proportion to their dominance by the capitalistic entrepreneur. The contrast between the experiences of the United States and Australia in the depression is significant. Australia got out of the depression quickly by taking unorthodox action through state and banking control; the United States got deeper into the depression by holding firmly to an orthodox course. This, I admit, is a sweeping generalization that requires close examination of the differing circumstances of the two countries. I point the contrast to emphasize a fundamental fact in recent economic evolution—namely, the increasing need for state action if capitalism is to continue to yield its best fruits.

This analysis may have simplified the basic problem of structural adjustment in the Western economy that was required to ensure ample scope for the enterprise of the entrepreneur, and which would at the same time have to provide in full measure for what may be called the overall development of certain basic natural resources by government initiative. The latter were required to strengthen the framework in which the private sector could develop efficiently and also to meet the increasing and, on the whole, legitimate demands for social betterment.

In differing degrees, the pattern of development in the Western economy has been based upon structural changes that increased the part played by public investment and also made greater provision for social services. The former would stimulate the rate of economic growth, but it may be doubted whether, in the more extreme developments of the welfare state, the latter has not in some cases impeded growth and impaired the vigour of the economy as a whole. It might reasonably be claimed that rates of growth today in the countries of the Western world are higher in those countries in which the government has undertaken much direct investment, or has participated in planning an overall high level of investment, and has at the same time pursued the objectives of the welfare state with some degree of caution. Low rates of growth tend to prevail where the welfare state has been developed to the point where social security ('security—mortal's chiefest enemy') is the prime goal of economic statesmanship, or where the collective pursuit of public investment has been neglected because it is politically objectionable, or where political leadership has not grasped the constructive contribution that the public sector can make.

Here again, the time-lag of ideas is the principal deterrent to the desired rate of basic economic progress, and we may well raise the question whether the relatively low rate of growth in the United States and the United Kingdom is not due to one or other of these forces.

The leading countries of the Western world that have had high rates of growth in recent years are Japan, West Germany, Austria, and Italy, the annual rates varying from 9·1 to 5·7 per cent in real gross product. It is true that these countries have had to repair the damage of war and that they have not had to bear the burden of armaments, but, on the other hand, they have devoted their energies to a planned growth, encouraged a high rate of saving, and avoided the extravagances of the advanced welfare state. There has, in short, been a high degree of co-operation between government and private enterprise in reaching a desired goal, but the basic structure of the economies is private enterprise. Given the appropriate milieu of leadership in the government as well as in the private sector, and a plan of action to pursue, a rise in the rate of growth—in a predominantly capitalistic structure—is thus possible. But here, as in any Western economy, the basic conditions of success rest upon some form of partnership between the public and private sectors, and the avoidance of fiscal policy that diverts resources into undue provision for social security facilities.

Social and Economic Policy as a Deterrent to Growth

The modern free-enterprise economy has to contend with three other problems that may slow down the rate of growth. These are: (*i*) the production of agricultural surpluses and the virtual abandonment of the free market in the sale of agricultural products; (*ii*) the growing influence of trade unions in some countries in demanding and securing collective agreements that provide continuous wage increases beyond the increase in productivity per man hour; and (*iii*) the fear of rising prices, now designated 'inflation'. As regards the third, the pursuit of a fiscal policy in the form of a credit squeeze, it is designed deliberately to check the rate of growth in order to reduce the impact of the so-called inflationary influences on the economy as a whole.

In all these cases there have been basic changes in the structure of the economy, the effect of which is to impede the rate of growth. The impelling motive in the first two cases is the political and economic power of the primary producers and the trade unions in ensuring rewards, both in excess of the net contribution to gross product and greater than would normally be available in a free market. This influence is not necessarily to be deplored. The basic and legitimate claims of social justice in a modern society cannot be determined by the play of the market alone. Under certain conditions, the political influence of groups like the primary producers could lead not only to a more equitable distribution of the gross national product, but also to increasing productivity in the sectors of the economy concerned. This depends, however, upon closer co-operation between the groups involved, including the government and the employers, in order to ensure that concerted action is taken (*i*) to promote productivity, (*ii*) to make the fullest use of advances in technology in all fields of enterprise, (*iii*) to promote administrative efficiency and co-operation among all sections of people working what should be a common enterprise, and, finally, (*iv*) to lay the foundation of a distributive structure designed to encourage greater equity in the sharing of increased returns ensuing from a greater productivity.

It is on this basis too that the bugbear of inflation, which has become somewhat of an obsession in many Western communities today, could be dispelled. In so far as action is taken to check inflation, it is mainly through fiscal policy that it inevitably reduces investment, impairs the rate of growth, and reduces the per capita return from the economy as a whole below what it could be if basic action were taken on the lines suggested above. It has been contended, among other things, that inflation falls with undue severity upon the recipients of fixed incomes and on the holders of fixed interest-bearing securities. There is a widespread view, moreover, that rapid expansion involving rising prices and a decline in the value of money also exposes the whole community to the risk of recession and unemployment, and perhaps even to a depression that may severely affect the incomes and employment of many people. Unfortunately, the measures taken in recent years in most of the Western economies afflicted by the fear of inflation have merely served to call a halt to development, thus placing the main burden of the adjustment on certain sections of the community, though relieving those on fixed incomes from the affliction of a decline in purchasing power.

No basic solution of the so-called menace of inflation has yet been developed, though action on the lines I have suggested could perhaps ensure that costs were held in check and increasing returns to individuals made to bear a closer relationship to advances in real productivity. With such a complex social problem, it would be unwise to assume that the goal of stability in the general price level is in sight in even the most enlightened free economy. It may well be argued whether the policies that have been implemented in certain countries in recent years have not, on the whole, involved a greater net cost than would have resulted from some rise in the general price level, by including a somewhat inequitable distribution of the costs of adjustment as well as impeding the rate of growth.

In many cases it is possible to ensure against the risk of falling purchasing power for those whose incomes remain relatively fixed in money terms. Pending the more constructive approach by government and private enterprise to develop, through co-operation, a concerted policy designed to ensure that the level of money income in the several sectors of the economy rises in close relationship with any increase in real productivity, it would be more economical to provide safeguards against the decline in purchasing power for certain income groups than to seek to control the price level by periodically resorting to a restrictive fiscal policy. Those who are obsessed by the perils of rising prices—and this concern, which is all too widespread, involves a questionable interpretation of the concept of inflation— might well pause to consider whether they can so readily alter the course of history, and also whether the burdens of rising prices have caused more affliction to modern communities than the disruption of falling prices.

What should emerge from this consideration of the basic problems—which involves promoting development with reasonable economic stability—is that no power groups should have the political or self-imposed right to demand more than their share of the national product. In this, as in other fields of social policy, the free economy can yield its best fruits only by the constructive co-operation of the public and private sectors in devising a policy that not only promotes rapid growth, but also imposes restraints on the sectors of the economy that seek returns in excess of national productivity or of their own individual contribution to gross product.

Collective Goods and Services

In recent discussions on the reconciliation of the objectives of rapid growth and economic stability, for example, in Sir Dennis Robertson's Marshall Lectures for 1960 (*Growth: Wages: Money*, Cambridge University Press), there is fortunately rather more emphasis upon growth as the prime objective, and a more balanced view is taken of the methods by which stability can be promoted than was the case two or three decades ago. I have given reasons for fostering a generally high rate of growth: the population bulge, with its immediate large increase in the work force and in the marriageable age group; the rapid rate of technological processes, emphasizing as they do the problem of obsolescence; the challenge of the communist economy; the aspirations of the underdeveloped economies. If the Western economy is to respond to this new situation, thrust upon an unsuspecting world, it will not be in the path of wisdom to assume that the play of the market alone in a free economy will achieve the desired result, any more than it would have produced the rapid developments in the welfare state in the past two or three decades.

As indicated throughout the previous all-too-brief discussion of this wide and complex problem, it will be necessary to devise a plan to reach a desired goal, and to contemplate a new and constructive partnership between the private and public sectors of the modern free economy. This is not something new and untried, as I sought to show in the paper read at the Harvard Tercentenary, in 1936, in the section concerning the part the State had to play over the years in making provision for 'collective goods and services' (see pp. 83 and 84 in the Appendix, 'The State and the Entrepreneur').

Planning for Growth

It may be that in some welfare states too much attention has been given to some forms of this state action. In the situation we have in mind at the moment, we are concerned with action designed to impart added vigour to the economy as a whole, to step up the rate of growth, to divert a higher proportion of gross product to investment, to seek to reconcile stability with growth, and to ensure as close a relationship as possible, in a growingly complex economic structure, between rising productivity and monetary rewards. For this purpose an overall national plan will be necessary, and it is no mere coincidence that the United Kingdom, the erstwhile cradle of laissez-faire and classical theory, should now be sponsoring the development of such a plan, or at least taking its first vital step on that road. Circumstances and emphasis will differ in different countries, but I repeat that the prime object should be to foster higher rates of growth than will be possible from undue reliance upon the play of the market in the private sector of the free economy.

I dealt with this problem as affecting Australia in a paper read before the Twenty-Sixth Summer School of the Australian Institute of Political Science in Canberra, 30 January to 1 February 1960. The topic for discussion, on which five papers were presented, was *Australia 1970 and Beyond*, since published by Angus and Robertson of Australia under that title. The topic allotted to me was 'The Economy: the Economic Potential and How to Achieve it.' After dealing with the problems and prospects of development in the decade of the sixties, I concluded by proposing 'A National Plan for Economic Growth.' I quote this plan, as outlined at the time:

These then are some of the basic developments that will set the pattern of economic growth in Australia in the decade we have now entered. It will inevitably be a decade of expansion at a greater rate than ever before in Australian history. The external picture favours this and, as already indicated, there are built-in factors in the Australian economy that will encourage expansion. But it will require national action to ensure a balanced development and the requisite rate of investment, both public and private. In short, it needs an overall plan.

In the minds of some people, the idea of a national plan in a free enterprise economy is heresy, savouring of undue government intervention and direction of private enterprise. The communist world has shown what may be done by conscious planning, and the countries of the underdeveloped world that are making the most progress are working under an overall plan. Why should the Western world shun the idea of a plan, especially when it is a plan for growth that is contemplated? I propose to conclude by outlining the essential features of a plan that will ensure a decade of rapid and co-ordinated growth, with the maximum use of resources of manpower and material and a rising standard of living. The essential features of such a plan might be stated as follows:

1. It will be necessary to step up the rate of public investment from its present figure of about 8 per cent of gross national product to perhaps 10 per cent. At current money values this would involve a public works programme of £A650 million, in place of the present figure of £A520 million. With increasing gross product this figure would rise annually, and might be £A800 million at current money values by the end of the decade. Unless this is done, the community will be constantly handicapped by inadequate supplies of the basic services supplied by public investment. This is the central feature of any such plan; it is the fundamental ingredient of ordered and rapid growth in the economy as a whole.

2. To make this need plain for all to see it would be desirable to set up what might be called a fourth estate of government, complementary to parliament, the executive, and the judiciary. Such an estate would be composed of elder statesmen without executive function, but required to report periodically to the Federal and State governments on the growing needs of the public sector for education and health facilities, water and irrigation, roads and transport, communications, power and fuel, and housing. It would also report on the population growth and the age distribution. Much of the material for such reports already exists in the records of public utilities and governments, and in their own estimates of the development that lies ahead for their particular enterprises. The public should be aware of the magnitude of the task that lies ahead, and governments given the encouragement and authority to carry it out in a co-ordinated attack.

3. To meet the cost of expansion it may be necessary to raise taxation to provide the necessary funds over and above what can be borrowed in the form of public loans. This would ensure the diversion of resources to investment from consumption, and act as a check upon the tendency of prices to rise. But, to the extent to which taxation was used for such purposes, it would be appropriate to give the taxpayer a bond bearing a low rate of interest and negotiable for certain purposes. Both the present and later generations would benefit by the development engendered by such a means of what would amount to a form of compulsory saving. In these circumstances, the taxpayer would be entitled to some compensation, and the country would be in a sound economic position to meet the cost.

Increased taxation devoted to development of the public estate would constitute a positive fiscal policy. This is already the case with the large proportion of public investment now financed from taxation. To speak of increased taxation being necessary to check a rise in prices is to miss the main point, constituting as it does a negative approach. The suggestion for combining increased taxation to raise public investment with the issue of a bond to the taxpayer gives both to him and the community as a whole the best of both worlds.

4. Apart from some more rigorous national control of hire-purchase arrangements, it would not be necessary to interfere in any way with the private sector of the economy, which could only gain by the more favourable framework of essential public services in which it would be operating.

The need for a national plan to sustain and increase investment is implicit in the first report (April, 1959) of the Manufacturing Industries Advisory Council, established by the Minister for Trade, the Hon. John McEwen, in July 1958. In dealing with the problems of investment, the Council emphasizes the need for an increase in private investment, and adds, 'At the same time, however, public investment must rise: the conclusion seems certain—we must plan for investment of a higher proportion of national income' (page 24). This is the primary task before the Australian economy in the decade ahead. It will demand courage and imagination in political and economic leadership of the highest order. For those who grasp the opportunities ahead and seek to proceed upon a well co-ordinated plan, the sense of achievement will be its own reward. Their contribution to national development will fully justify any special measures needed to ensure the appropriate allocation of resources between investment and consumption as a whole, and between the relative rate of growth in the public and private sectors. An appropriate motto for those who guide economic policy could be:

Cras ingens iterabimus aequor. (Tomorrow we set out once more upon the boundless sea.)

I shall not elaborate on this text except to say that the concept of the fourth estate was designed to serve the double purpose of drawing public attention to the basic problems ahead and of offering to both public and private authorities suggestions of the broad lines on which economic policy might be developed. It should be emphasized that the fourth estate would have no executive authority, nor would the governments be obligated to implement its report or recommendations, but it would be desirable that the reports be published so that the people as a whole, and those with executive responsibility in both public and private enterprise, would be informed of the considered views of a body established to make continuous surveys of the state of the economy, and of the measures by which the public and private sectors could co-operate in constructive action to reach the desired goal. In outlining the plan I had in mind the major problem of growth, and this is most important for Australia because of its still vast empty spaces, its need to build population as rapidly as possible, and its geographic situation, close to the world's most densely-populated area. If problems of stability as discussed earlier in the lecture arose, as they would inevitably in an expanding economy, the responsibility for examining them and reporting upon them could readily also become a function of the fourth estate.

II

PUBLIC ENTERPRISE: ITS GROWING ECONOMIC AND SOCIAL SIGNIFICANCE

In the first lecture, attention was drawn to the growing importance of the public sector in the modern Western economy and to the emphasis that was being placed upon public investment. This is one of the fundamental transitions that is taking place in the Western economy, and there is little doubt that it will be even more important in the development of the underdeveloped countries now aspiring to modernize their ancient peasant economies. As I shall be referring frequently to the underdeveloped as compared with the developed countries, I propose to use a special nomenclature for the sake of brevity and clarity. I shall refer to the developed countries as D_1, and the underdeveloped as D_2. With the possible exception of Japan, the D_1 countries are members of what might also be termed the Western economy.

Public Expenditure and Gross National Product

It is not generally realized that most of the D_1 countries have a government expenditure on goods and services amounting, on the average, to about one-third of national income. This is due in part to the emergence of the welfare state and to the emphasis in recent years on social security and expenditure in the social services. But, in many countries in recent years, the public sector has also entered into the field of investment and development on a greater scale, owing in part to political emphasis upon the nationalization of some industries, and in part to the growing importance of transport, power and fuel, water conservation and irrigation, and education and health, which in many countries have been regarded as appropriate fields for public enterprise. In the aggregate, leading countries of Western Europe collect in revenue, through taxes and services rendered, a much higher proportion of gross national product than is generally realized.

These and other important points concerning the growing significance of the public sector are emphasized in the *Economic Survey of Europe 1959*, published by the United Nations' Economic Commission for Europe. This shows that the proportion of government receipts to gross national product was between thirty and forty per cent for Austria, Finland, Germany, the Netherlands, Norway, the United Kingdom, and Sweden, with Italy and Denmark between twenty-five and thirty per cent. Thus, for good or for ill, with such a large percentage of gross national product being absorbed in total government receipts, the public sector has an important impact upon the economy as a whole. The high proportion of government receipts is due to a variety of factors; mainly, essential expenditure on national services, such as education and health and defence; the expanding provision of social services; the liquidation of debt incurred in wars; and an increasing tendency in some countries for governments to assume certain responsibilities for economic development. One important fact that emerges from the study to which reference has been made is the substantial contribution made by the governments of some countries to gross savings. Thus Table 3 in Chapter V, p. 8, of the *Economic Survey* gives the following figures of gross savings of governments:

GROSS SAVING OF GENERAL GOVERNMENT
DURING THE PERIOD 1950–58

	As percentage of gross product	As percentage of gross saving
Finland	12·1	45
Austria	7·3	35
West Germany	7·2	27
Luxembourg	7·9	26
Norway	7·0	26
Portugal	2·9	25
Netherlands	5·7	23
Denmark	3·9	22
Sweden	4·8	22
United Kingdom	2·9	18
Italy	3·8	18
France	2·4	13
Spain	2·2	21

Note. The figures in this table do not cover the whole period 1950–58 for all countries, but varying numbers of years within the period.

These and other figures all serve to demonstrate that the public sector has in recent years assumed an importance that is perhaps not fully realized. Indeed, except for some recent studies, it may be claimed that the economic significance of the public sector is perhaps a somewhat neglected field of economic study and research. This is all the more surprising in view of the fact that in a little over three decades since 1914, the Western economy was involved in two world wars of greater magnitude than ever before and in the most pervasive and severe of all depressions. In each case there had to be some overall government policy, increasingly impinging upon the free play of markets, and centrally directed allocation of resources. With the rise of the communist economy to a vigorous force in the world and the efforts of the D2 countries to adapt their ancient economies to modern industry, agriculture, transport, and power, the public sector in the West is inevitably on a much greater scale than in the heyday of the free Western economy at the turn of the century.

These changes are due not only to developments in political thought and action, especially the emphasis upon social services and social security through the development of the welfare state; they also recognize the fact that, in some cases in the modern technological developments of industry, action on some concerted plan, on the national scale, may prove to proffer the most economical use of available resources. Apart from these internal changes in the Western economy itself, there is also to be considered the impact of development of economic policies and action in the D2 countries and the measures that have to be taken by the D1 countries in rendering them economic aid. This will require, on the part of governments of D1 countries, collective action to an increasing extent, if they are to build a constructive nexus with D2 countries and are to give to the West a new and expanding field for leadership in the world economy.

The Scope and Function of the Public Sector

In considering the part now played in varying degrees by the public sector in the Western economy, it is necessary to distinguish the several spheres in which public enterprise has assumed leadership and control. It is necessary to emphasize again that the sphere of the public sector varies among Western economies: in some of the western European countries, where the welfare state and nationalization have been more fully developed, it has a large and varied function; in the North American economy, where greater significance is attached to the private sector as providing not only the mainspring to action, but also the most appropriate and economic allocation of resources, it plays a less significant role. But the overall picture is one of an increasing share of both operation and control passing to the public sector. In a greater or lesser degree the public sector is now responsible for a number of key operations in the control and development of all Western countries. These may be stated as follows:

1. The provision to an increasing extent of basic facilities for transport and communications, such as

roads and ports, telegraphic, telephone, and cable services, airports, and, in many countries, air services and
railways. In a rapidly growing world economy, with
increasing emphasis upon technological change, the
rate of growth of these services must be higher than the
growth of the economy as a whole. To a greater degree
than hitherto, it is necessary to contemplate co-ordinated
plans to ensure their most economic operation. Not only
has the public sector been playing an increasing part
in this field, but the prospect is that this must go on at
perhaps an accelerating rate.

2. A second field of growing significance for the public sector is the provision of power and fuel and of water
and irrigation for both industry and agriculture in all
countries. For a country like Australia this is already
very important; with modern technology, the rapidly
increasing population in most countries, and the development of new demands for many resources, this
field of public enterprise is bound to be of greater
significance generally and to emphasize still further the
need for public investment in economic development.

3. Of no less importance is provision for research,
education, and technical training. The state in most
countries has played the key part in providing these
facilities; and, with the current developments in technology and population growth, it will be necessary for
all countries to contemplate a rapid expansion of their
enterprise in this field. The private sector will no doubt
continue also to make an important contribution in the
universities and technical colleges, and in its own research work relevant to the particular operations of the

company concerned. But it is clear from recent experience, as well as from the trends indicated for the immediate future, that more and more of the responsibility must fall to the state. It is not so merely through the demands of a technological age; on the population front the significant relevant fact is what may be termed the 'younging' of nearly all populations. The age groups fourteen to nineteen and twenty to twenty-four in the next two decades will grow at a much greater rate than the population of most countries as a whole. This is due in part to the higher post-war birth rate in most countries, but also, and perhaps of greater significance, to the conquest of lethal disease—what may be termed 'death control'. It is not only that world population is bound to increase at an unprecedented rate, with a reasonable prospect of doubling by the end of this century, but that, in the immediate future, the greater increase is likely to take place in the younger age groups.

If adequate education and training are to be offered to these increasing numbers of adolescents and to the marriageable-age group, the traditional facilities will have to be greatly enlarged. This task will fall mainly to the lot of the public sector, and increasing resources will have to be made available for this purpose. It may well be doubted whether any Western country today has adequate plans to meet this problem. The task ahead is not merely to do justice to the growing numbers of young people, but to ensure that the asset they represent as an expanding work force in a highly technological age is not wasted. Perhaps no task before either the public or the private sector is more important or more rewarding—in the widest sense of the term.

4. Then there is the impact of taxation upon the economy of the modern state. This opens up a many-sided problem, and one on which it is not always easy to get an unbiased opinion. The fact is, however, that a large proportion of gross national product in most countries is taken in taxation by governments and local authorities to meet the costs of the increasing responsibilities imposed upon governments by modern democracies. Here are some relevant figures giving the percentage of taxation to gross national product in representative countries for 1959:

United States	17·9
France	16·4
Sweden	19·5
Canada	12·3
Italy	14·8
Germany	16·1
Norway	18·0
United Kingdom	22·4
Australia	17·0
Austria	23·6

(Based upon statistical material in United Nations publications, with special reference to the *World Economic Survey, 1960* and the *Economic Survey of Europe in 1959*.)

This gives an average of nearly eighteen per cent, which may be taken as broadly representative of the whole Western economy. The collection and spending of so large a proportion of gross product inevitably has the double impact both of greatly influencing the distribution of real income and of playing an important role in the allocation of resources. This raises crucial questions concerning the economic significance of both the altered distribution of income and the consequent change in the allocation of resources. These questions cannot be answered on grounds of economic considerations alone; the broader social effects based upon what may be termed concepts of social justice must also be taken into account. Here again it is doubtful whether leading countries in the Western world have given these problems the attention they deserve. The assumption usually is that taxation is too high; it is the impact upon the taxpayer that is most consciously felt and noticed. The question arises, however, whether the impact upon the economy as a whole is not more important; whether the expenditure has not been more beneficial socially and economically, than if the funds appropriated by the tax gatherer had been allowed to 'fructify' in the pockets of the taxpayers!

Fiscal Policy as a Weapon of Control

Finally, it is necessary also to consider the whole impact on the economy of fiscal policy in the broad sense, both long and short term. To an increasing extent in all countries the banking system has come under official control, extending beyond the original concept of the central bank established as a semi-independent authority to control monetary policy and to ensure exchange stability. Official fiscal policy in recent times has assumed a much more comprehensive control of monetary and banking operations in many countries, with the objective of reconciling high rates of growth, the pursuit of full employment, and the provision of increased social services with economic stability— especially stability of the price level. Measures have been taken, more often under direction from the government than by the independent action of the central bank, to control the proportion of reserves to the deposits or to the advances that the trading banks should hold. In this way, a credit squeeze has been applied from time to time to check the tendency of prices to rise—but also at the expense of checking the rate of growth. The following table gives the rate of growth in gross product for the countries listed in the previous table, in the decade of the fifties, and the rise in prices for the period 1953 to 1959.

| | Percentage increase in g.n.p. at current prices | | Prices indices for 1959 based on 1953 at 100 | |
	1951–1955	1955–59	Wholesale	Consumer
United States	20·4	21·2	108	109
France	40·4	51·2	126	129
Sweden	28·2	28·9	108	120
Canada	28·2	28·0	104	110
Italy	35·4	30·1	98	113
Germany	49·1	38·5	105	92
Norway	28·9	25·8	111	120
United Kingdom	31·3	23·4	106	120
Australia	37·6	27·5	105	116
Austria	51·5	34·2	114	115

(Based upon statistical material in United Nations publications, with special reference to the *World Economic Survey, 1960* and the *Economic Survey of Europe in 1959*.)

The causes of rising prices are of such an intangible and complex nature that any solution attempted through credit control might well miss the issue. In any case, there is no close correlation between rising prices and rates of growth in gross national product, as the preceding table shows.

In applying fiscal policy designed to check the rate of expansion, the objective has also been in many cases to correct the balance of payments without recourse to the more direct method of imposing import restrictions. Whatever be the object of the restrictive fiscal policy, the fact is that the banking structure as a whole has been subject to increasing government control, and this in turn has given the public sector of the economy increasing influence over the private sector. As regards the fear of inflation and the use of fiscal measures to seek to control it, the *World Economic Survey 1960* has an interesting passage reviewing the relative importance of growth and stability, and the measures taken in recent years to attain stability, as a prime object of economic statecraft. I quote the following extracts from p. 7 of the report, to indicate that the pursuit of stability by policies of restraint, so far from achieving the main objective, may in some cases aggravate the situation. In a word, it is not possible to build a nation on a credit squeeze.

This point bears emphasizing because cases in which governments have succeeded in achieving high rates of growth together with price stability are frequently cited as evidence in support of the thesis that restraint of demand to keep prices from rising will not interfere with the rate of growth. But the issue is not whether there is a positive rather than a negative correlation between rates of growth and rates of change in price. A rapidly growing economy may, through the stimulus it provides to high rates of investment, technological innovation, and increasing productivity, be more conducive to price stability than is a sluggish economy. Thus, the issue is not whether economic growth and reasonable price stability are in principle irreconcilable. The issue is rather whether a conflict between the two goals may arise in fact if price stability is pursued by a policy of restraint of demand regardless of the degree of slack in the economy.

This concentration of public thinking and public policy of recent years upon the danger of inflation is now coming to be increasingly challenged by the thesis that the main danger to the economy lies in an inadequate long-term rate of growth, and that the risk of inflation is not so great as to require a policy of restraint upon aggregate demand while there is yet so much slack in the economy. This currently developing reorientation is visible in the United States Administration's diagnosis of the need for policies to achieve not merely recovery from recession but also long-term full utilization of productive resources. It is even more evident in its proposals for investment in human and natural resources, as well as for the stimulation of investment in plant and equipment designed to increase the rate of growth of the potential levels of production and employment. If this reorientation has been correctly diagnosed, an expansion of the rate of growth of the United States economy might well be expected.

Such a growth-oriented policy, it may be noted, does not necessarily mean sacrificing price stability and embracing inflation. Rather, it involves a shift in the methods of fighting inflation, from primary reliance on measures to restrain demand to the inclusion of policies designed to accelerate the rate of expansion of incomes and the available supplies of goods and services. In a world in which inflationary pressures are so largely the result of mutually frustrating attempts of various income-earning groups to increase their respective shares of the national product, it is not unreasonable to expect that an increase in the size of the total share to be divided will contribute to some relaxation of the pressure. To the extent to which an increase in prices results from a larger rise in wages than in productivity, the stimulus to output per man that is imparted by higher investment and a higher rate of growth of national product may very well slow down rather than accelerate the rising trend in prices.

The Public Sector and the National Objective

This survey of the several forms of public sector activity and control which have been developed in the past three decades, in varying degrees by all the Western economies, should leave no doubt that the so-called free economies of the West can no longer be regarded as demonstrating the virtues of the untrammelled play of market forces under laissez-faire.

In Chapter V, Part III, of the *Economic Survey of Europe 1959*, the Secretariat of the Economic Commission for Europe draws attention, perhaps for the first time in an important international publication, to the economic significance of the public sector. Referring to the fact that in most countries of western Europe about one-third of the national income is channelled through the public sector and that government expenditure on goods and services and public investments absorbs from fifteen to twenty-five per cent of gross national product, the report states, 'Hence the way in which the public sector operates is bound to affect significantly the course of economic development.'

It is perhaps surprising that this fact has not been given much more prominence in economic discussions, whether in the university lecture room or in the halls of parliaments. There has been far too great a tendency, especially in the North American economy, to disparage the part played by the public sector, and to assume that any decline in the scope of its operations would *ipso facto* be in the best national interests. So far from the public sector declining in importance, there is every reason to suppose that the development in the infra-structure of the Western economies in the immediate future is likely to increase the relative part played by the public sector. At least that is the inevitable con-clusion, from the brief survey given here of the scope and nature of government control and operation in the modern economy and of the predominant economic trends for the years immediately ahead.

What has to be contemplated is a more positive approach in building a constructive nexus between the public and private sectors, in a concerted effort to increase the rate of economic growth, to promote higher productivity in the economy as a whole, and to allocate resources in such a way as to ensure that, in both the long and the short term, economic activity will enrich the quality and variety of national life. This naturally involves greater understanding by the people, as well as by the leaders of public and private enterprise, of what the end of economic activity should be, and what forms of resource development and organization of the economy will be in the best national interests. The 'adventure of development' is thus not merely a matter of developing resources on the basis of rapid technological advances, but of blending this higher return for economic effort with the broader and more subtle objective of improving the social structure of the nation as a community. On this point I quote the closing paragraph of an address which I gave to the Sixty-Fifth Annual Congress of the Agricultural Bureau of South Australia in Adelaide in July 1958, and which was published in a volume of essays on the Australian economy under the title *The Adventure of Growth* (Cheshire, Melbourne, 1960).

The time has come to take stock of the position on a national basis. The problem ahead can be clearly outlined as regards population growth and its age distribution; the claims of expanding education and health services; the requirements of fuel and power, transport, water supply and irrigation; the lessons that scientific advances have to offer the man on the land; the need for continued research, the investment needs of public and private enterprise for an expanding economy; and the respective responsibilities of Commonwealth and State governments and industry. Our objective should be to seek a basis of co-operation in sustaining our expansion and in meeting the increasing claims it is bound to make on our resources. No individual section could succeed without a plan based upon a correct interpretation of future prospects and an assessment of the resources available to meet its problems. How can we expect to get the best fruits of the opportunities ahead for the nation as a whole without a global plan? How can we expect to understand the nature of the problem without such a review? This is surely the beginning of wisdom in any enterprise. Action on these lines would enrich the adventure of development and give to the community a sense of common destiny.

The Need for a National Plan

It is perhaps no mere coincidence that I should be preparing these lectures on the changing structure of the Western economy at a time when the United Kingdom is announcing a fundamental, and somewhat revolutionary, proposal for a national plan, to be developed by the government in co-operation with the leaders of the employers and the trade unions. I referred to this problem in the first lecture and quoted from a suggestion I had made early in 1960, for the establishment of a fourth estate of elder statesmen to survey

periodically the state of the economy and to suggest broad measures of policy that would ensure the appropriate economic and social adjustments to the rapidly-changing economic scene in all progressive economies. The Chancellor of the Exchequer in the United Kingdom has now proposed the establishment of a National Economic Development Council (N.E.D.C.) to be based partly on the experience of the French *Commissariat du Plan*, which has played a key part in developing plans for the French economy and in reconciling the aspirations of different industries. Though the Chancellor will himself be Chairman of the new Council, it will have no executive function. It will be a semi-independent authority composed of representatives of employers and employed, with perhaps some independent members, and charged with the responsibility of establishing what the essential conditions for realizing potential growth are.

Whilst this is not as radical a proposal as the suggestion for a fourth estate, with independent authority to report upon the state of the economy and make suggestions on major policy issues, it is a striking departure from the long-established practice in England of remote democratic control over basic decisions of the Cabinet and from the strongly-entrenched position of treasury and civil service officials in their relations with Ministers of the Crown. The new proposal does contemplate the appointment of a full-time working staff under the control of a director appointed from outside the civil service, to report upon the state of the economy and to make recommendations to the new Council for its consideration. The effectiveness of such an arrangement would turn in part upon the degree of independence the staff and its director felt able to exercise in reporting to the Chancellor and on the willingness of the Chancellor to submit reports to the Council, even when they might conflict with declared government policy.

The London *Times* of 9 October 1961, in a leading article referring to the status of the staff of the new Council, remarked that 'it must, of course, be a Government body if it is not to run counter to Government policy.' But it added that 'it must also, like the French Commissariat, establish an independence of its own.' These issues remain to be resolved, but the proposal to contemplate some form of national planning in basic economic policy for the United Kingdom is an encouraging departure from traditional practice; to be welcomed as a new approach to the overwhelming problem that faces not only the United Kingdom but all the countries of the Western economy.

Planning and the Adventure of Growth

In the Storr Lectures at Yale University in 1958, the distinguished Swedish economist, Dr. Gunnar Myrdal, dealt more fully than most economists with the development of the control and direct activity of the modern state, as well as with the urgent need for a comprehensive plan to co-ordinate state activity and to promote a more constructive partnership between the public and private sectors. This is necessary not only within the Western economies themselves, if they could be considered in isolation, but even more so in their relations with the underdeveloped countries and for meeeting the challenge of the planned economy in communist countries. We shall deal with this problem in some detail in Lecture III. It should, however, be emphasized, in considering the place and function of the overall state plan in the free and advanced economies of the West, that a well-constructed plan would not of necessity involve more detailed control and intervention by public authorities. On the contrary it should mean less, especially if the plan embraced the task of co-ordinating the operations of all the public authorities, local and central, and gave more emphasis to the place of the public or statutory corporation in the public sector.

As indicated in the first lecture, the statutory corporation, if well conceived and given the appropriate degree of independence, neatly blends the virtues of public and private enterprise. It has a recognized and clearly defined public obligation to discharge, but its board of control is free, or should be free, to develop the structure and operations of the corporation with imagination and vigour. It may well be that in the future development of the Western economy there will be greater scope for the statutory corporation, as indeed is certain to be the case in the D2 countries, where a much greater proportion of development will fall to the lot of the public sector. On this an extended quotation from the Myrdal Yale Lectures, published under the title *Beyond the Welfare State* (Duckworth, 1960), pp. 28–9, provides a convenient summary of the main thesis I have been seeking to develop:

My account of the internal forces behind the trend towards planning in the Western countries would be incomplete if I did not conclude by pointing specifically to the urge there for continually rising levels of investment and production, incomes and well-being. In this particular respect people today in the Western world are not different from those in the other two orbits. In the very first paragraph of the Preface, I referred to what I believe is a fact, namely that, in spite of the chasms of ideologies and the wide gaps as between the three orbits in level and modes of living and working, we are all existing in the same era of civilisation, with a considerable and growing unity of basic ideas and ideals. One such congruity of thoughts and strivings is the dynamic conception implicit in our thinking about the national economy. In all countries we are now striving for 'development'.

This is most emphatically the case as far as the poor nations are concerned, as they become aware of their low economic levels and form the ambition of raising them. When they insist upon being given the designation of the 'underdeveloped' countries— instead of the static one, more commonly used in earlier times: the 'backward regions'—they want to characterize themselves as needing development, and being bent upon achieving it.

In the Soviet Union of the Seven-Year and Five-Year Plans and in all the other countries within the Soviet orbit, people have been living, and are now living more intensely than ever, in an orgy of climbing percentages, symbolising the rise of every level in the economy. The development targets are spelled out in individual production plans splashed at the entrance of every factory and on the walls in the meeting-room of every collective farm. Within the country, within every region and, indeed, within every enterprise, 'socialist competition' makes the fulfilment—and preferably the overfulfilment—of the targets a concern to every manager and every worker. In relation to the outside world, the targets represent a constant race with the capitalist world, a race of momentous, fateful, and almost religious import.

III

THE CHALLENGE OF THE
TRI-PARTITE WORLD

IF it be true, as has been suggested in the two preceding
lectures, that new situations developing in the Western
economy itself demand new approaches and new policies
to affect the relative parts played by the public and
private sectors, the global change in the world economy in
the last three decades reinforces this basic thesis. No
doubt it is still one world in the sheer physical sense, but
it operates in three main parts. The great problem before
mankind is to find the basis of co-operation that will at
one and the same time satisfy the aspirations of the two
new sectors in the world economy, and replace the
present international tensions that dominate the world
scene by new techniques of constructive association,
designed to promote the welfare of mankind as a
whole. This is the greatest challenge that has ever con-
fronted the human race, involving as it does the development of a world economic and social order. The
new system must be capable of meeting technological
change and population growth at an unprecedented
rate and of imparting order and a sense of unity, at the

international level, to what is at the moment a tri-partite structure, inclined to dwell too much upon its differences and too little upon developing common action among all three divisions.

The Western world is by design and consent, though sometimes under pressure, surrendering its colonial domination over vast areas and numbers and thus creating the new underdeveloped world stretching literally from China to Peru. It is aspiring to recon-struct its political and economic life to the demands of self-government in varying forms, modern industry, and agriculture. In the meantime, there has developed the new communist sector of the world economy, inspired by an intense devotion to modern technology in all fields of enterprise, and already demonstrating a capacity for economic growth in basic industry that more than matches the rate of growth in the more advanced, mixed economy of the Western world. Despite its totalitarian political structure and its en-slavement—in a new form of colonialism—of over one hundred million people, with a considerable historic and cultural heritage, in parts of central and eastern Europe, it would be a mistake to assume that the people of both Russia and China do not feel that they now have a new sense of adventure in their economic plan-ning and development.

The West has established communities that blend, better than ever before, high and rising standards of productivity in all fields of enterprise with the egali-tarianism of the welfare state. But it now faces the double challenge of the rapidly growing economic power

of the communist world and of the new and commend-
able aspirations of the underdeveloped world to
modernize its ancient peasant economy and provide
higher living standards for its rapidly expanding numbers.

Apart from meeting the more immediate challenge
of the communist economy, with its concentration on
basic industry and its high rate of economic growth, the
Western economy must give consideration to the ways
and means by which it can assist the underdeveloped
countries. They have a much more difficult task of
combining the reconstruction of their economies with
some noticeable and satisfying increase in their low
living standards. It is estimated that in the decade of
the fifties, the national income of the underdeveloped
countries rose by about three per cent per annum, but
the population rose by two per cent per annum, so
that the increase in income per head was of the order
of one per cent, or in money terms about one dollar per
head. Meanwhile, the increase per head in the United
States was $23.50, and in the countries of the Common
Market in Europe, $20 per head. Thus the gap be-
tween living standards in the developed and underdeveloped countries is widening, a situation that is not
conducive to building a new sense of community
between them.

The Growth of Population

The problem is, of course, complicated by the problem of population growth, the impact of which is much
more acute in the underdeveloped countries. All popula-

tion estimates made in recent years tend to give higher and higher rates of growth. In 1925, the population of the world was of the order of 1,900 million, and in 1960, it had reached approximately 3,000 million, an increase of about sixty per cent in thirty-five years. This was a much greater rate than ever experienced before, but the estimates for the years immediately ahead give even higher rates of growth. Thus the figures furnished by the United Nations now suggest totals of over 3,800 for the world in 1975 and 6,250 by the year 2000 A.D. On this estimate, the increase in the last forty years of the present century will be over one hundred per cent. This is in itself a major problem for the world as a whole, but when the figures are considered for the different groups of countries, the problem is even more challenging. The following table illustrates this point. It gives estimates of population for North America, Latin America, Asia, and Europe.

ESTIMATED POPULATION IN MILLIONS

	1960	1975	2000	Percentage increase 1960–2000
Africa	235	305	517	120
North America	197	250	312	60
Latin America	205	310	592	190
Asia	1,615	2,220	3,870	140
Europe (including the U.S.S.R.)	635	755	947	50

(Based upon statistics from *The Future Growth of World Population* published by the United Nations Department of Economic and Social Affairs, 1958.)

In this table, North America excludes Mexico as part of Latin America. It demonstrates that the greatest increase in numbers will take place in the underdeveloped countries, already overpopulated by Western standards. This makes the task of the underdeveloped countries all the more difficult in adjusting their economies to the more advanced standards of the Western economy and to the new and vigorous upsurge of the communist economy in the development of modern technology. At the same time, the growth of population emphasizes the importance of the Western economy entering into a more energetic and constructive partnership with the underdeveloped countries in their plans for economic and social development.

I shall deal with this problem later; meanwhile it may be of interest to contrast the growth in world trade as between the developed and the underdeveloped countries (D1 and D2) in recent years. Taking imports as a suitable measure because of the urgent need of the D2 countries for modern equipment and capital goods, the total of world imports rose from $75,900 million in 1953 to $117,700 million in 1960, an increase of fifty-five per cent. The imports of the D1 countries rose from $54,400 million to $88,400 million, an increase of sixty-three per cent. The imports of the D2 countries rose from $21,500 million to $29,300, or only thirty-six per cent, despite the greater relative increase in population and the pressing need for a higher rate of economic expansion. The greatest increase in imports was by the Common Market countries, from $14,920 million to $29,590 million or ninety-five per cent, followed by

Japan, with a rise of eighty-six per cent, to $4,491 million in 1960, and Australia, with an eighty-two per cent increase, to $2,367 million. As an indication of the magnitude of the problem, Australia, with a population of a little over ten million (though increasing at one of the highest rates in the world), had a level of imports nearly one-tenth of that of the D2 countries, with a population more than one hundred times as great.

For some years, in the United States and elsewhere, I have sought to emphasize the urgency of greater aid for the D2 countries, and in what follows I quote the full text of an unpublished address given to the United Nations Association in Adelaide on 21 August 1958. It may repeat in some particulars the argument already advanced on this problem, but if it was true in 1958, it is much more relevant to the world situation now.

Challenge to the Western World

Three facts make the problem of the underdeveloped world of great importance to the Western world and to the future of the United Nations. First, the growth of population will involve a tremendous increase in the numbers inhabiting the already overcrowded countries of the underdeveloped world. Secondly, the aspirations of many countries in the underdeveloped world, with their new sense of nationalism, lead them to reconstruct their ancient economies and to plan for rising living standards, despite the increasing numbers. Thirdly, the communist world has been developing plans for economic aid to a number of countries in the underdeveloped world and it is now in a position to increase this aid whether in terms of equipment or technical assistance.

The Economic and Social Council of the United Nations has itself developed techniques for providing aid and, through its agencies such as the Food and Agricultural Organisation, the World Health Organisation, the Technical Assistance Board, and the International Labour Office, has contributed substantially to promoting international co-operation in a field that affects the economic and social life of people in the underdeveloped areas. The questions we must ask ourselves are whether enough is being done; whether the Western world is concentrating too much upon military alliances and not enough upon the constructive work of economic and technical aid; whether we may not be faced with a situation in which the poor will become poorer and the rich richer; and whether this won't defeat our basic objective in securing an enduring association between the underdeveloped world and the Western world, to the detriment of the communist world.

These are serious questions and should be pondered by all who seek to establish the prestige and effectiveness of the work of the United Nations. For example, take the following figures: in the industrial nations of the West, with less than twenty per cent of the population of the world, the total gross national product (i.e. the goods and services available per annum to the people) is about two-thirds of the total gross national product of the world. In the underdeveloped world (including China for this purpose), with about two-thirds of the world's population, the total gross national product is less than twenty per cent of the world product. In the industrial nations of the communist world, with about fifteen per cent of the population, the gross national product is slightly less than twenty per cent of the world product. The proportion of the total gross national product accruing to the industrial nations of the communist world is increasing, and so is the proportion accruing to the Western world. This is not true of the proportion accruing to the massive numbers of the underdeveloped world, and this, I suggest, is one of the key problems facing the United Nations. Moreover, it provides the ground upon which fruitful international co-operation can be developed.

In the post-war period, some steps were taken indicative of an understanding of this basic problem. In our small way we in Australia can take pride in the beginning of wisdom, as concerns our own geographical position, by enunciating the imaginative Colombo Plan. On a much grander scale, our American friends have led the Western world out of the wilderness of the devastation of war by the foreign aid of UNRRA and the Marshall Plan and subsequent economic and technical assistance. There is nothing in history to equal the generosity and magnitude of this global aid. But in this world of rapid change and growth, we cannot afford to dwell on the past—not even the immediate past. Our time-lag must be adjusted to the shortening of the time-lag in technological and political change in the world around us, and to the lengthening of the time-span of life, to the extraordinary phenomenon of death-control that is giving the whole world—and especially the underdeveloped world—the greatest and most rapid increase in population in all history.

At present rates, the population will double before the end of the century and most of the increase will take place in the so-called underdeveloped world, for the most part among Australia's neighbours immediately to the north. Whilst this massive increase in numbers is occurring, the countries concerned, having recently resumed their ancient role as independent states, will be engaged in an heroic effort to modernize and industrialize their economies, in the light of technological advances and through the incessant demands of their expanding numbers.

This, I suggest, is the point at which the common interests of the countries of the Western world are the most pressing and offer the best opportunities for fruitful co-operation. For us in Australia, it is vital that we should build an association of mutual respect with our neighbours in South and East Asia. For the United States, with the hand of destiny upon it as leader of the free world, there is the great responsibility of piloting a new course, in which the resources of the Western economy will be available on terms of mutual trust to the underdeveloped world, in the gigantic task that it now must assume. Much has already been done through the Colombo Plan, the Technical Aid Programme of the United Nations, the Food and Agricultural Organisation, the World Health Organisation, and direct economic aid to many countries. But in recent years a new situation has developed. On the one hand, the challenge of time makes it imperative that a new and more constructive approach to the whole problem be initiated in order to build a new bridge between the Western economy and the underdeveloped world, to promote expansion that could not but benefit the free and the underdeveloped worlds alike, and to counter the threat now developing from the communist world.

We are far too apt to look on aid as a cost, and to ignore the constructive political associations that it will yield and the benefits of economic expansion that will inevitably follow. We have the example before us of the United Nations Relief and Rehabilitation Administration, that did so much in all devastated countries immediately after the war and was abandoned all too soon. This was founded on a pro rata contribution of all Western countries willing to participate. Why not adopt a similar procedure for a comprehensive and constructive plan of economic and technical aid to the underdeveloped world, to assist in its present efforts of adjusting its economic structure to modern techniques and of building better living standards for its massive numbers? This would, at one and the same time, elevate the prestige of the Western world and provide an enduring basis for the expansion of the world economy, at a rate that could not but benefit contributors and recipients alike. It would also promote the basic work of the United Nations.

For this purpose, a contribution, by all countries willing to participate, of not less than one per cent of national income per annum for a period of five years to a special United Nations fund for economic development, would have the double advantage of raising the prestige of the United Nations in the uncommitted world and of providing a basis for an expanding world economy. The fund so established would be available to meet the present contributions being made to the Colombo Plan, to the Technical Aid Programme, and to other agencies of the United Nations. But there would be a substantial surplus over these commitments which could be used to give the underdeveloped countries the opportunity of proceeding with their plans for economic reconstruction. The cost to the contributing countries would not be unduly burdensome and the return, whether in economic terms or in building an enduring political association with the recipient countries, would in the long run far outweigh the cost. If administered through the United Nations and its agencies, there could be no question of political pressures being exercised or of special favours being meted out to particular nations. Nor would there be the fear that any one of the contributing nations would call the tune.

Thus we could expect new and fruitful relations to be built with the less fortunate countries, who face baffling problems of increasing numbers and economic reconstruction on a great scale. At the same time, the foundations would be laid for an expanding world economy capable of meeting the challenge of population growth and the conflict of ideologies. If the West resumed its leadership on this imaginative basis, it would be living up to the historical challenge it now has to meet and following the advice of a recent statement from the

United States that came to my notice: 'We should stop telling the world what we are *against*. We should tell the world what we are *for*.' In such an enterprise the countries of the free world would find ample scope for constructive co-operation in high endeavour.

New Partnership with Underdeveloped Countries

Economic aid to the underdeveloped countries, on the scale of not less than one per cent of the gross national product of the United States and Canada, the countries of Western Europe, Australia, and New Zealand, would provide an annual contribution of approximately $9,000 million, rising by from three to four per cent per annum with the growth of the Western economy. This would increase by some forty to fifty per cent the amount now provided; even more, if the proportion provided for military assistance were reduced in relation to that for purely economic and social development. In addition there would be the flow of private capital for investment in the underdeveloped world, now approaching some $5,000 million per annum.

It should not be assumed, however, that a global sum of this order is the answer to the problem that confronts either the Western countries or the underdeveloped countries in building a new association between them. The problems are far more complex than the provision of a given sum for economic aid. It is true that these problems cannot be solved without such grants from the more prosperous countries of the West, but to use these grants in the best interests of both the Western economy and the underdeveloped economy will require a global campaign for the successful adaptation of the social structure of the underdeveloped countries to a new way of life. This will involve developing a new and constructive partnership between the more advanced Western world and the Eastern world, now imbued with the new spirit of adventure in modernizing their ancient economies and social organization. Moreover, the much more difficult and elusive problem of developing the technical and educational facilities of the rapidly increasing populations in the countries receiving aid has to be faced. Should a partnership develop, these countries could assume that they will be able to rely, to an increasing extent, on their own resources; they could thus build new and independent communities, capable in the not-too-distant future of carving out their own national destiny, both economically and socially, as members of an expanding world community.

This would be perhaps the greatest and most noble enterprise the human race has ever contemplated, and the most rewarding. The communist world could not ignore such a challenging experiment, either in terms of economic reconstruction or as a new association in promoting the ultimate human values among the world's teeming millions. If the West embarked upon such an experiment, it could call on all good men and true to come to the colours; to give less prominence to bi-lateral aid—with its doubtful political and military implications—and to strengthen the United Nations, and its agencies, in its most difficult and important task of building a new economic and social structure in the countries most in need of aid. For the West, as can be demonstrated, this whole venture would not be a cost but an investment, in the broadest and most rewarding meaning of the word.

The Shape of Things to Come

In 1960, the newly established American Assembly of Columbia University published a book under the title *Goals for Americans*, which was the report of the President's Commission on National Goals and was prepared by a group of distinguished American scholars and men of affairs. The report should be an essential part of the stock-in-trade of all people in the West who are concerned with the shape of things to come and with making some constructive contribution to developing what is in the best interests of the prestige and valour of Western democracy.

At the close of their report, the Commission published a table giving their estimate of the possible developments in gross product in the three sectors of the world economy in the decade ahead. The table (Table II, p. 369 of *Goals for Americans*) is reproduced on page 58. The figures are given in U.S. dollars, and naturally the average rates of growth assumed for the several countries in the sixties represent an informed judgement that may well be subject to error.

SELECTED PROJECTIONS OF GROSS NATIONAL PRODUCT

Orders of magnitude only

	Estimated 1960 total (billion $)	Assumed 1960–70 rate of increase (%)	Estimated 1970 total* (billion $)	Resulting 1960 per capita in $	Resulting 1970 per capita in $
Advanced free nations					
United States of America	500	40	700	2,800	3,400
Great Britain, France, Western Germany	175	40	250	1,200	1,600
Rest of Western Europe	115	40	160	650	850
Canada, Australia, New Zealand	55	50	80	1,800	2,200
Japan	35	55	55	350	500
Sino–Soviet bloc					
U.S.S.R.	225	70	380	1,000	1,500
European satellites	80	60	130	800	1,200
Communist China	90	100	180	130	210
Less-advanced free nations					
Near East (including Greece, Turkey and Egyptian part of U.A.R.)	22	60	35	185	225
South Asia	40	60	65	75	100
Free Far East (excluding Japan)	25	60	40	100	130
Africa	30	60	50	135	170
Latin America	50	60	80	250	300

* Sources: 1960 data derived from best available published estimates, principally from Congressional hearings. All estimates in 1958 U.S. dollars.

The report makes the following comment upon this table:

Table II uses these general estimates as a basis for projections of the possible situation in 1970. The data for 1960 are derived from published estimates, principally as presented to committees of the U.S. Congress by responsible Administration officials. To derive per capita output figures from the projected totals, UN population projections (on the 'medium' basis) have been used.

The result is *not* to be interpreted as a precise forecast. This is particularly so for comparisons between the U.S. and U.S.S.R.; even if the GNP projections were numerically accurate, a realistic comparison would focus rather on the allocation of resources for key national uses, where the gap is much narrower, and on living standards, where the gap is wider.

But there are three important conclusions concerning the coming decade to be drawn from Table II. These conclusions are 'broad brush' but nonetheless so clear as to withstand any reasonable adjustments that might be required in particular figures.

1. In terms of total production and per capita income, the U.S. and the major advanced free nations will continue to have the capacity for rising living standards and adequate defense, and will have increased capacity for assistance to the less advanced nations. Total product will be substantially greater than that of the Sino–Soviet Bloc.

2. By 1970 the Soviet Union will have further consolidated its status as an advanced nation, with the capacity to support a major military effort, to increase the living standards of its people, and also to engage in far more extensive foreign economic activity. The same is true of the European satellites, which must be considered instruments of Soviet policy. Communist China presents a different and unique picture with strong and growing elements of contrast. Rapid industrialization may well bring output in key areas, such as steel and electric power, within reach of the stated goal of surpassing Great Britain, though its technology will not be up to Japanese levels. Communist China may be well on the way to becoming the dominant industrial power of all Asia, surpassing Japan and India.

On the other hand, low per capita output will still require Peiping to concentrate heavily on internal development; in effect,

Chinese leaders themselves concede this when they speak of the many more years, after this decade, needed for 'building socialism'. This does not diminish one whit the psychological and practical effect on Asia of Communist China's material advance, but it does define limits to what Communist China will have achieved. It will be a nation 'advanced' in a few formidable respects, but with overall rounded development still distant.

3. The nations included in the 'less advanced' category, both individually and in any conceivable grouping of common economic and political purpose, will remain well behind the advanced nations. The average per capita figures are a general indication of their continuing need for capital. This will be true to some degree even in the exceptional cases of Israel and Venezuela; it will most assuredly be the case for such major nations as India and Brazil, which will have per capita products of the order of $100 and $250 respectively.

The Concept of a World State

In physical terms, the gulf between the probable living standards of the advanced free nations and the less-advanced world, including China, during the extended period required for the latter to make their basic adjustment to an economy which will absorb and fully utilize modern technology, presents a forbidding problem. The West will continue to enjoy the fruits of decades of development and of educational and technical advances, and its more prosperous sectors will probably continue to outstrip the rate of growth in income per head of the less-developed countries.

In these circumstances, the latter may appear to be fighting a losing battle and the former, enriching themselves in giving aid to their less favoured associates. This is an apparent dilemma in the early period of this proposed partnership between the haves and the have-nots;

the possibility of overcoming it would lie chiefly in the faith that moves mountains and in the long-term assurance that the fruits of victory will reward the enterprises of those—in both the more favoured and the less favoured countries—who would have the courage and foresight to embark upon such a magnificent venture.

My distinguished predecessor in the last series of Beatty Lectures, given here at McGill earlier this year, spoke of the early Chinese and Roman Empires as world states—not merely in the literal, geographical sense of embracing the whole habitable and traversible surface of the planet. Actually, they co-existed on its surface for several centuries without colliding with each other, and indeed without being more than dimly aware of each other's existence. A future state would have, by contrast, to be literally world-wide, now that modern Western technology has knit up the whole surface of the planet into one military area. This geographical point is, however, a superficial one. On the political and psychological planes, the Roman Empire and the Chinese Empire were authentic world-states. They were authentic because they solved the human problems that make a world-state at once difficult to build and indispensable to have. These historic world-states imposed peace on varied communities, that had been perpetually waging war on each other, before they were fully deprived of their sovereignty and independence. They succeeded in subordinating and uniting the lesser states. In the second place these world-states eventually won for themselves the loyalty of the liquidated states' former subjects. They inspired a common veneration and affection in the hearts of populations that differed from each other in race, language, culture, and religion.

These two achievements in the sphere of human relations are all that we have to ask of a state that would be literally world-wide. It is reassuring to recall that the necessary political unity and psychological solidarity, that are for us now the alternatives to self-destruction, have been achieved in the past on at least two occasions. Both the Chinese and the Roman world-states were successful in giving peace and order to millions of human beings for centuries on end.

Basic Social Adjustment in Underdeveloped Countries

In terms of distance, transport, and speed of communication, the world today is one in the physical sense, more than ever before. The Western world, as the leader of technical and democratic development over the past two centuries, has produced a political structure blending economic proficiency and social welfare on a scale unparalleled in history. It is proceeding to withdraw, voluntarily or under pressure, from its imperialistic ventures in the underdeveloped countries, which are now imbued with a new sense of their national destiny. This offers the scope and opportunity for these two societies to join in a common effort to found the basis for a world state, dedicated to the complementary tasks of bringing the fruits of modern technology to hundreds of millions of people and of spreading its benefits in terms of social justice, on a scale greater than ever before.

This would be bringing the new world into action in a new sphere, to redress the balance of the old. As already suggested, this cannot be done by direct economic aid alone, though this is a basic condition of the success of the whole enterprise. There must be the development of modern capital equipment in the less-developed countries, but its full fruits will only be realized if there are, at the same time, quite profound changes in their social structure. In particular it will be necessary to have a substantial degree of literacy and the development of a cadre of well-educated and technically proficient people, capable of grafting the democratic progress and technical achievements of the West on to the social and economic structures of these older countries.

Secondly, and more difficult, it will be necessary to promote in the less-developed countries a more substantial measure of social justice, in terms of economic betterment for the masses, as opposed to the present situation with its feudal landlords, usurers, grasping merchants, or profit-hungry proprietors of new industries. This involves a revolutionary social adjustment, a breach with the way of life of the underdeveloped countries established over the centuries; it will not be achieved without patience and understanding by those in the Western world.

In the third place, the whole administrative apparatus, in both public and private enterprise, will have to be transformed in the D2 countries, with the emphasis on the former sector. Whilst private enterprise should have scope for its development and for the contribution it can make to the new aspirations of the underdeveloped countries, it should be realized that, as concerns certain basic facilities of modern economic development, the emphasis upon the public sector will necessarily be greater in the underdeveloped countries than in the Western economy as a whole. Indeed it may be claimed that, on both social and economic grounds, public enterprise in certain basic industries offers better prospects for effective and acceptable economic development than private enterprise. If it is true, as now seems likely, that the advanced countries of the West require an overall national plan to sustain and promote their own economic growth, it is much more the case with the underdeveloped countries. Their urgent need is for what may be called a Planning Development Authority, to provide inspiration and guidance for a balanced programme of both economic and social adjustment to modern technology. This could promote the partnership required between the advanced and less-advanced countries for full fruition of the latter's potential.

Adventure in Development

This is a formidable task for both parties, but for the Western world it offers the prospect both of a new and rewarding political association with more than half the population of the world and of an expanding economy on an unparalleled scale. It would enable the Western world to resume leadership in economic and social development and to bring new hope to the growing numbers in countries with low living standards. The West has pioneered the development of modern techniques, as well as initiated the egalitarian features of the modern welfare state. It is therefore in a position to guide and assist the underdeveloped countries along the same path and in the process to enrich its own experience, in both economic and human terms.

With the existence of such a partnership between the developed and underdeveloped countries, the communist world, now advancing at a rapid rate, would be under challenge to blend its own achievements and growing power with a new world order, dedicated to the task of diverting economic resources and the productive power of a technological age to the betterment of mankind as a whole. This may be regarded as a vision splendid, not capable of being attained. But with the new sense of common purpose among the European countries of the West and their close association with the United States, and with the new Commonwealth of Nations which supplants the British Empire, an international political structure is being developed capable of embarking upon so bold an adventure. Moreover, the United Nations has developed a wide range of agencies, through which technical aid and guidance on the broad social issues could be made available to the underdeveloped countries on a multilateral basis, free from all suspicion of desire on the part of the advanced countries to seek political or territorial power over those to whom aid was being rendered. It is true that new vigour and a greater sense of adventure would have to be imparted to the United Nations and its agencies, if so vast a problem were to be handled with any assurance of success.

Andrew Shonfield, in his penetrating book, *The Attack on World Poverty* (Chatto and Windus, 1960), has dealt fully with the issues involved. If economic and social planning has come to be recognized as a basic condition of successful economic growth and the attainment of social welfare in the so-called free democracies of the West, how much more important is it on the international front? On this point I quote the brief closing paragraph of Shonfield's book:

All this would help to enhance the authority of the United Nations on matters which go far beyond technical assistance. Its successful conduct of a difficult relationship with the governments of underdeveloped countries would establish it in a new position of trust. One way or another, governments have got to get used to dealing with the United Nations as an effective supranational body, if the world is to survive the next hundred years. Success in this task of economic leadership in the underdeveloped countries would make a useful start in preparing the right habit of mind.

The Future of the Entrepreneur

In conclusion, may I refer you to a brief passage on the problem from the Harvard paper of 1936, the paragraph on p. 85. This excerpt explains how, despite the emphasis upon the public sector in a new world economy embracing social and economic development in the underdeveloped countries, there would still be great scope for the private sector. The entrepreneur would have an overall national and international function of greater magnitude than ever, and would occupy a key position in an expanding world. Without a question of a doubt, it is imperative for him to grasp the urgency of the situation and to rise to the challenge that destiny presents him with; to do this, he will have to arm himself with more knowledge, dedication, and conviction than he has ever required in the past.

APPENDIX

THE STATE AND THE ENTREPRENEUR*

THIS subject is on the frontier between economics and political philosophy. It contains problems that cannot be solved by economic analysis or abstract philosophy alone. There is still much unknown territory in which no one can speak with the authority of the scientist. Judgment and belief have a wide influence. In what I say this morning I am influenced by my judgments of what has happened in many countries in the recent past and by my belief that in the immediate future important developments will occur in the relation of the state to the entrepreneur.

Let me summarize my thesis. The function of the entrepreneur must continue to be performed in any community that desires to make progress. The qualities of imagination, leadership, and adventure necessary for great constructive work were exercised by the entrepreneur under free capitalism. During a large part of the nineteenth century he was left free in most countries to pursue his objective of maximum profit without serious interference by the state. This was true especially of the United States, where even in the post-war period (1919–1929) capitalism flourished and its virtues were extolled as never before in the history of man. Then came the great depression to expose the grave defects of an economic order that had no solution for economic fluctuations and no means of ameliorating the burdens of depression. Capitalism under the control of the entrepreneur guided mainly by considerations of maximum profit is now completely discredited. It does not give economic security to the masses of the people; it does not provide the administrative machinery whereby increased technical efficiency is transformed easily into a generally higher standard of living; it does not furnish society with the social institutions required to meet the strains imposed by economic fluctuations and

* Reprinted with the kind permission of the Harvard University Press from *Authority and the Individual*, Harvard Tercentenary Conference of Arts and Science (Cambridge, Mass., 1937), pp. 48–73.

rapid technical progress; it does not provide the increasing range of free or collective goods that enter more and more into the standard of living. Countries have been able to absorb the shocks of depression and improved technique in inverse proportion to their dominance by the capitalistic entrepreneur. The contrast between the experiences of the United States and Australia in the depression is significant. Australia got out of the depression quickly by taking unorthodox action through state and banking control; the United States got deeper into the depression by holding firmly to an orthodox course. This, I admit, is a sweeping generalization that requires close examination of the differing circumstances of the two countries. I point the contrast to emphasize a fundamental fact in recent economic evolution—namely, the increasing need for state action if capitalism is to continue to yield its best fruits.

The Private Entrepreneur not as Important as We Think

There is one point on which we should clear our minds at the outset. The capitalistic entrepreneur occupies much less territory than we think. In all European countries and in some British dominions the state is entrepreneur over a large field of industry —water-supply, communication, some forms of transport, lighting services, education, public health, certain forms of banking and the supply of credit, housing of the poor, road construction.

Every rise in the standard of living, every increase in the complexity of economic organization sooner or later forces the state to assume control or ownership of natural monopolies, of the supply of collective goods (such as education, health services, libraries), of the provision of services that would cause ruinous competition under free enterprise. The principles underlying this extension of state control are well understood and accepted in most countries. To a visitor from a country which had long ago gone far in this direction, the controversies over state control in the United States appear a little unreal. They show that unfettered capitalism will die hard in the United States, as it did elsewhere. I believe that it must die if the United States is to build up an industrial structure that will provide both social security and economic well-being. The problem is one of reconciling the authority of the state with the free play of individual enterprise in a wide though diminishing field of industry. The early enthusiasm of the New Dealers has perhaps obscured the view of this fundamental problem. It is well to start a steep climb in low gear. You have been in high gear for three years, and you may feel the need of relief from machine-gun legislation.

In a reaction against state interference it is tempting to think of the entrepreneur as being the driving force in economic progress. In all countries, even in the United States, governmental or semi-governmental bodies plan and carry out a substantial proportion of new development. In Australia it is much more than 50 per cent, and in Great Britain it is about 50 per cent. Public investment accounts for half the total new development. In some European countries the proportion is higher, culminating in nearly the whole of investment in Russia being under the direct control of the state. This is highly significant. The state has devised administrative machinery with which, in an increasing range of industries and services, it can and does perform the functions of the entrepreneur. This is perhaps the most striking change that has taken place in the economic system in the present century. It has been accompanied by the development of administrative machinery by the state and by an increasing emphasis upon the social responsibilities of the entrepreneur. The rise of the state as entrepreneur is a direct challenge to individual enterprise and its methods.

Under undiluted capitalism the typical industrial entrepreneur works through the joint stock company. This is a form of group control which has its own bureaucracy and its own administrative methods of reconciling initiative and authority. But in its extreme form it recognizes few social responsibilities and no fixed obligations to labor or capital. 'I owe the public nothing,' recently declared a great American entrepreneur. This is an extreme example of individualism. Many cases of entrepreneurs taking the opposite view could be given, but it is well to remember that joint stock enterprise by its very organization may, and frequently does, take its social responsibilities lightly. In times of depression the lower rate of profit becomes the standard rate of dividend throughout industry; the reduced volume of employment, the accepted rule. By devising the principle of the equity share and by assuming the right to 'hire and fire' labor, joint stock enterprise gets the maximum freedom of action with the minimum social responsibility. This must be summarily rejected as an unsatisfying ideal, though many economists have sought in the past to rationalize and justify the behavior of the entrepreneur when he acts in his own right to

pursue his objective of maximum profitable output without regard to the social effects of his action.

The State Commission as Good as the Joint Stock Company

The state as entrepreneur has found difficulty in devising an appropriate administration. Where, as in the United States, it had limited its intervention largely to control, it devised the regulating commission, which left the entrepreneur free to manage and develop his enterprise within certain broad limits. In a country that retains its faith in individual enterprise, even in public utilities, there is great scope for the development of this form of control. Perhaps this will be the distinctive contribution of the United States to the problem. In countries where the state or public authority has assumed ownership of an increasing range of industries, it has devised administrative machinery not unlike joint stock. The state now hands over the enterprise to a board or commission with complete powers in internal management and the right of initiative in development, though not necessarily full financial powers. There are many examples already of this machinery, e.g., the Port of London Authority or the State Electricity Commission in my own State of Victoria. There is no reason why the state should choose its board less wisely than the average joint stock company which is controlled by directors selected from the hierarchy of finance found in every modern industrial center. If the commission has full powers and the untrammeled right of initiative, it should give results not less satisfactory than those of the joint stock enterprise. But where, as in many cases of state enterprise in Australia, Parliament retains the right to plan and develop the enterprise, there is wide scope for mistakes and financial losses. Parliament must delegate its authority, retaining the right to lay down general policy and to call upon its commission for guidance and information. The fear of parliamentary control, itself often irresponsible in industrial enterprises, competes with the social irresponsibility of the entrepreneur in deciding whether an industry shall be state-owned or not.

The state as entrepreneur encounters two obstacles which do not beset the path of the capitalistic entrepreneur in his pursuit of maximum profit. The first is publicity. The state enterprise must do much of its ordinary work and all of its planning and development in the full light of day. It must give information when asked

and offer explanations that hamper both expedition of decision and effectiveness of action. But this is, on the whole, a good thing. The capitalistic entrepreneur would often pause if he were forced to explain his action and to discuss the social disturbances caused by rapid changes in technique initiated by him. Many do hesitate before plunging whole areas into distress, but many are powerless against the new processes or new industries created by a young and enterprising generation of competing entrepreneurs. In a world where, as Professor A. N. Whitehead has remarked, the changes of generations are now concentrated in a single lifetime, anything which reduces the rate of change of scientific technique until social administration makes up some of the leeway is probably a net economic benefit. But this would not be the case if our social administration were inspired by the fire and imagination of the inventor and the successful entrepreneur. The world is richer in material things than it thinks, and it will be richer still. Its progress is retarded by timidity, by confusion of ideas, and by conflict of interests in social administration. Nothing is more striking in the modern world than the contrast between the entrepreneur's devotion to the material benefits of scientific progress and his distrust of improved methods of social administration. The one appeals to his idea of progress; the other offends his sense of freedom. Yet it is clear that the entrepreneur cannot himself utilize the rapidly improving technique science holds out for him unless the state provides the administrative machinery through which social organization can be adjusted to improved processes of production. The state as entrepreneur must reconcile its social responsibilities with its desire to adopt more efficient processes. The individual entrepreneur cannot do this if his competitor takes immediate advantage of the improvement.

The control of finance in state enterprise gives rise to the second obstacle which the state as entrepreneur encounters. Experience shows that an increase in public investment is inevitable. The proportion of public to private investment will increase. This means that the proportion of fixed to equity debt* will increase. The state raises its funds on fixed interest-bearing bonds. So does the local

* Fixed debt is a fixed capital sum, often with fixed interest, such as debentures, government securities. Equity debt is a debt which fluctuates in amount and interest with the fortunes of the enterprise. Shares are the common examples.

body or the semi-governmental authority. The state is expected to meet the interest on the whole of the debt in season and out of season. The joint stock company, on the other hand, has an equity debt to deal with and can vary dividends according to the prosperity of the company or the general prosperity of the country. There is, moreover, much capital lost in joint stock enterprise; no one knows how much, and no one knows what is the average rate of interest earned on the total capital laid out in joint stock enterprise. I can only raise the doubt whether it is 4 per cent, which we may accept as the average rate of interest that the state may have to pay on its debt. If the state extends its functions as entrepreneur and fails to earn 4 per cent, as I think it inevitably will, the balance has to be made good from taxation. This is a levy on the community in order to maintain a certain rate of interest which may be out of harmony with the real earning capacity of industry.

The problem is likely to become very important. The state will be encouraged to borrow and to extend the proportion of fixed interest-bearing debt. With the increased demand for economic security and the greater capacity to save, more and more savings will pass into the hands of institutions like insurance companies, trustee companies, and savings banks that invest predominantly in the gilt-edged bond. As the demand for this form of investment expands, and the scope for it is enlarged with the extension of state enterprise, it becomes less and less a sound investment. Unless the state is prepared to tax its people for the benefit of the *rentier* the investment loses its gilt. The alternative is to establish some form of equity in a portion of the debt, so that the interest varies according to the prosperity of the country. This change will be resisted by financial entrepreneurs, but short of a periodic scaling-down of the interest burden, or its counterpart in a moderate dose of inflation, some extension of the principle of the equity-debt to state enterprise appears to me inevitable. Widespread demand for economic security through savings and investment in fixed interest-bearing bonds creates a new financial problem. It is not possible for the whole community to insure itself against risks. The greater risks are those of contraction of enterprise and deflation. No country since 1928 has suffered from taking a modest dose of inflation. Countries that have administered it have prospered most. The fear of inflation is a confession of inability to control banking and financial policy. Without this control sound administration

of the modern economic system is impossible, if only for the reason that fixed debts become too burdensome.

Supplanting Price as the Regulator in Primary Production

Thus far I have assumed that the state was supplanting the entrepreneur in large-scale industries and that there was very little change in the organization of the industry. It is surprising how state enterprises have copied the capitalistic technique, even to the practice of advertising a virtual state monopoly. There are essential differences in finance, social responsibility, and publicity, but not in the technique of management. State enterprise is relatively easy in these fields, and its logical extension may take place in transport, insurance, banking, supply of standard goods.

But in recent years the state has been driven into another field where the difficulties are very much greater and the conflict between the state and the entrepreneur likely to be much more drastic. I refer to the intrusion of the state into the regulation of output, prices, and finance in primary industry. The impelling motive here is the increasing pressure from the primary producers for economic security. There is, on the one hand, their desire to be protected from normal cyclical fluctuations in prices. No system of insurance against this risk has been effectively designed by individual enterprise. The elimination of the risk of 'normal' fluctuations in prices, normal in the sense that they represent the ordinary business cycle, would rather strengthen the primary producer in his discharge of the entrepreneur's function. But control does not stop at the reduction of these price fluctuations. It goes much further and has derived great stimulus from the depression, which has emphasized the effects of 'the pace of progress' in commercial farming in the new world. We have seen in the last five years the long-period decline in prices of certain primary products caused by improved technique and increased acreage in new countries. To benefit by this capacity to produce primary products at lower cost, the world must allow prices to fall until a new equilibrium has been established between prices and production of primary and other products, with consequent writing-down of capital values. The state is justified in attempting to regulate conditions so that the adjustment will be less disturbing. But it has everywhere in the world gone much further than this. It has sought in the Old World to protect peasant agriculture by duties and prohibitions against

imports of cheap products, or by establishing elaborate machinery for controlling marketing and prices, as in the British schemes. In the New World many experiments are being tried—the 'domestic' price, direct bounties, destruction of some output, elimination of some areas of production, adjustment of farm debts. Some of these measures may merely retard adjustment, and this is quite a reasonable protective action against sudden and disturbing change. But many of the measures, if successful, would deny the world the benefits of cheaper goods, maintain effete methods of production, establish a cramping form of control, and destroy the initiative of the entrepreneur. Primary industry is in the hands of numerous small entrepreneurs. Control schemes must reach down into the intimate life and thought of these *paysans*, and limit the scope for the exercise by the individual of skill and initiative. They thus have the double disadvantage of keeping prices higher than is really necessary and impairing the efficiency of the entrepreneur.

The state may act as entrepreneur, it may compel the entrepreneur to observe certain conditions when discharging his own functions, but it cannot reconcile rigid control of market conditions with free exercise by the entrepreneur of his own functions. The state through its marketing board dismisses market price as an agency of control in favor of its own price. The individual entrepreneur will adjust his activities to this price, and soon production and price will be out of balance. The state must then abandon its control of price or set up control of output. This is the present dilemma of control schemes, but the state usually shrinks from the task of rigid regulation of output. It is difficult to secure the cooperation and acquiescence of the farmers necessary to push it far enough. It will be easy enough to establish and protect a monopoly in importing countries and to give the local farmer a favorable price. But this means stopping progress, not merely retarding it, and it throws the weight of adjustment upon the new countries where the entrepreneur has pioneered the way in commercial farming at relatively low costs. This is an alignment of economic forces that cannot endure. The state is not something external to the people comprising the state. It cannot permanently deny a benefit to its consumers or thwart the efforts of the successful entrepreneur. It cannot impose the necessary discipline on thousands of individual producers.

Unfortunately, the primary producers in new countries have

not grasped the significance of the lower costs of commercial farming. Like the farmers in the Old World, they too sigh for pre-depression prices and resist the contraction of the frontier necessary to restrict output to the profitable areas. For the time being they join with producers in the importing countries in a fruitless effort to combine maximum output and maximum price and to get the best of all possible worlds. Such striving after the unattainable must end in failure. There will be protection of agriculture in Europe and higher prices and increased production; there will be co-operation and control of producers in new countries for grading products, research, and reducing the costs of marketing; but if farming is to be carried on by the individual entrepreneur the rigorous marketing schemes and price controls will be preserved in name only. We have not yet devised a satisfactory halfway house between the state or collective farm and the individual entrepreneur in agriculture.

It is of interest to note that the schemes of state control of agriculture have in the main drawn upon the experience of the cartel. On account of the number and the dispersion of the entrepreneurs, the state has been used as the agency of control. In Australia we have for a long time used the device of 'the home price' behind import duties against foreign supplies. Butter is our classic example. We subsidise butter producers by this device to the extent of about £4,000 per annum. New Zealand is experimenting with a system of guaranteed prices in the same industry and is using the power of the central bank to inflate credit to pay the guaranteed price when world prices are low. Later, when the world price rises, it will be possible to deflate credit. This is a workable device, provided the datum price is not higher than costs on the average farm and there is a rigid observance of the scheme when the market price exceeds the datum price. The United States has gone further in the cartelization of agriculture by its scheme of compensating producers for reducing output and its long range plan of shifting or eliminating the marginal producer. But every country is alarmed at the reduction of the proportion of its people engaged in agriculture, when it should in fact welcome such a change. There is a common resistance to the cheapening of primary products, though a general welcoming of lower prices for finished products.

Apart from the resistance of the farmer to change and the general rigidity of the structure of rural industry, there is an additional

influence at work retarding adjustment to new conditions. This is the method of financing agriculture. During times of depression there is a constant conflict between the mortgagee and the mortgagor. The former struggles to maintain the value of his fixed interest-bearing loan, the latter to preserve some of his equity in the enterprise. There is no automatic adjustment of debt burden to the varying fortunes of agriculture as there is in industry where the equity debt prevails. In times of major reorganization the resistance of the debt structure to change can only be overcome by somewhat drastic moratoria and state schemes to adjust the burden of farm debts. It is all very cumbersome and disturbing. Perhaps the best way the state can help the entrepreneur in agriculture to perform his functions satisfactorily and to respond to technical changes is to devise some more elastic system of financing agriculture. Doubtless the state could develop a form of equity debt for the large number of producers under its control at present, leaving private enterprise to follow its example or evacuate the field in favor of the state.

The State a Bad Loser

The state has been forced to enter the field of agriculture and to attempt some form of regulation of the entrepreneur largely for the same reasons that it has entered other fields, for example, the control of monopoly. It must provide reasonable economic security and preserve the economic order against the ravages of rapid technical change. These are largely negative actions. The negative aspect of state control or supplanting of the entrepreneur may be pushed too far. On the one hand, the state may be left to deal with the social problems created by the entrepreneur; on the other hand, the state may attempt too vigorously to retard progress. The entrepreneur should be encouraged to assume greater social responsibility for his own actions; the state must endeavor to promote the rapid and easy absorption of improved technique and efficiency in industry into a higher standard of living and a greater consumption of collective goods of the higher order. I believe there is wide scope for fruitful state action along both lines, and that the state of the future will spend more and more of its energy in positive action to promote a flexible economic and social structure. But the state can do only what its citizens want it to do, and the average citizen dislikes being disturbed.

The extension of state control and ownership is not, however, to be contemplated lightly. The state is a bad loser and by no means a good employer. It easily falls into the bad habits it deplores among entrepreneurs. Thus it is ready to use its powers to protect a monopoly, when it has one, to support high prices, and to use freely the weapon of price discrimination. All these were formerly regarded as cardinal sins of monopoly. Examples of these lapses into despised capitalist ways are numerous—e.g., where the state owns railways and has sought to cramp new forms of transport, where the state has acted in the interests of a special group of producers, such as coal owners or agricultural producers or highly protected manufacturers. As an employer we have had many examples in Australia of the state's seeking to deny its employees the facilities of wage-fixing tribunals which have complete control over industrial relations in private enterprise. Again, the state has not scrupled to use its sovereign powers to push nationalistic aims, just as the individual entrepreneur will exercise to the full his powers to push his individual interests. Much of the economic nationalism of the modern world is made possible because the state has used its powers regardless of the international complications that follow the pursuit of narrow national policy. Finally, I repeat that the state is a bad loser in the sense that its capacity to cut its losses is usually much lower than that of private enterprise. State enterprises when unsuccessful are politically hard to liquidate. Their position is allowed to drift, as we in Australia know to have been the case with some costly experiments in land settlement and irrigation. If the enterprise should be stopped when failure is apparent there would remain a debt to meet. This unhappy prospect deters a firm and prompt withdrawal, and so allows the experiment to be continued in spite of cumulative losses. The net result is a greater burden of debt and a discrediting of state enterprise.

Social Responsibilities of the Entrepreneur

With these strictures upon state enterprise in mind we must proceed cautiously in recommending any extension of it. What are the grounds upon which the state should assume greater control? If the individual entrepreneur meets his social responsibilities with reasonable efficiency it is better that he be left in occupation of his present industrial territory. He will then be fairly free to allow his

imagination to conceive new plans and methods, to indulge his spirit for adventure to his own satisfaction and to the benefit of the community, and to contribute to the advancement of thought and culture in his own individual way, as in the past. What are the social responsibilities he should recognize in the performance of his economic function? He should be able to offer reasonable security of employment to his men, or regard the provision for unemployment caused by industrial change as one of the costs of industry. He should establish, under control or otherwise, reasonable working standards. Wages should move up with improved efficiency and technical progress. Investment should not be recklessly pursued in industries already fully capitalized. The entrepreneur should be willing to continue to assume risks when depression threatens to supervene on prosperity, and he should be prepared to pioneer the way in the production of new goods made possible by improved technique and a higher standard of living. The dismissal of labor and the race for liquidity that mark the conduct of the average entrepreneur in times of doubt and impending depression are the negation of his social responsibility. They throw heavy burdens upon the state and discredit an economic system. In these days when men are massed in great industrial cities, the state is forced to assume the responsibilities that the entrepreneur has evaded, or to establish forms of control, such as industrial tribunals or national insurance, that will enable the entrepreneur to discharge his responsibilities. In the end the entrepreneur will be superseded unless he devises a technique for dealing with such a situation. Capitalism's lament may become a posthumous dirge.

This means that the entrepreneur of the future will perform his function within a framework of control that has been developing rapidly in many countries over the past three decades. Where the entrepreneur plays an important role his thinking dominates society. Much, therefore, depends upon how he thinks. But there is a conflict in the entrepreneur class as between the *rentier* and *entrepreneur* (enterpriser) proper. The latter deals with economic enterprises requiring planning and constructive administration. He comes closely into contact with human interests, and his social responsibilities are likely to be more present to his mind. The *rentier*, on the other hand, must constantly think of the liquidity of his assets and the necessity for meeting his fixed obligations (bank

deposits, insurance claims). He forces the pace in times of difficulty and relaxes control when things are easy. It is against him that a revolt in thought has occurred in the United States. He has lost much of his authority in Great Britain, where the industrial entrepreneur has come to dominate the stage since the mistake in monetary policy in 1925. The Premiers' Plan in Australia was, as much as anything else, an effort, and a successful one at the time, to force the *rentier* to accept his social responsibilities. Much of the agitation against banking under private enterprise is a protest against the failure of the *rentier* to discharge his social functions. Those banking systems will endure which recognize social obligations and submit readily to some form of control. But this is only one of the examples of the increasing scope of economic control in the future.

What form will this control take? The insistence on minimum standards of working conditions and wages is now familiar in most countries and is accepted as a general rule of industry. In the United States there is now proceeding a great controversy over this development of state action. I cannot comment in detail on this controversy and shall merely remark in passing that regulation of minimum standards in industry is on the whole in the best interests of the entrepreneur in countries that have developed a system of regulation. True, regulation of industrial conditions reduces the flexibility of costs, but it establishes a norm about which there is little dispute save in times of emergency or increasing productivity. In Australia the leading wage-fixing tribunal, the Commonwealth Arbitration Court, revised the basic wage downward in the depression, but only after lengthy inquiry. It has since raised it, but not yet to the pre-depression level. Where confidence in a tribunal is established, its findings are accepted and much controversy and conflict avoided. The establishment of some form of control of industrial conditions is a major controversy in the United States. You may work out a voluntary system typical of your industrial genius, but whatever form it takes, control will reduce the sovereignty of the entrepreneur, and in his own interests.

I pass to consider other aspects of control that raise questions less settled in theory or practice. They are (*a*) the claim for economic security, (*b*) the regulation of investment, and (*c*) the provision of collective goods and services not possible by private enterprise. All these may be shown to be essential to the building

of an economic order that will use to the full, progress in science and invention without causing social disturbance, while at the same time providing the conditions that will enable the entrepreneur to continue his work in the more restricted field in which he now operates. In a word, they imply that the capitalism of the future will be preserved by social controls. We are justified in making the old aphorism run: He who is not a 'socialist' at twenty has no heart; he who is *not* a 'socialist' at forty has no head.

The Claims of Economic Security

Take first the question of economic security. Even if the economic system were freed of the losses and disturbances of periodic depressions, unemployment caused by industrial change, sickness, and old age must be insured against. Much has been done in many countries to provide through private or state schemes for security against these risks of unemployment. The experiment of national insurance and old-age pensions in Great Britain is now perhaps the classic example. This is almost certain to be followed in other countries; some have already partial schemes in operation. But these schemes require state action, and they demand on the part of the entrepreneur a readiness to recognize the risks of unemployment and to contribute towards a solution. It is true that in the long run industrial progress benefits all the people. It is equally true, as the classical economists insisted, that invention in machinery will ultimately increase the demand for labor, perhaps at higher wage rates and shorter working hours. But this 'long run' means a relatively long period of unemployment for many workers directly affected by the decay of old methods of production. No scheme of insurance against this unemployment is practicable unless it covers a wide area, so that the costs of liquidating the old methods can be charged to the new. This is indeed one of the costs of progress. The entrepreneur must be prepared to assist in meeting these costs, whether he does it through a direct contribution to the unemployment fund in England, or an indirect contribution through special taxation, as in some states in Australia, or again as a special levy for public works, as in some European countries. I need not labor the main point. It is sufficient to draw attention to the failure of free enterprise to meet the situation. It is one of the situations that must be met in the future if the entrepreneur is to survive the criticism that will be leveled against him. We were forced to

meet it in Australia by special measures during the depression; and we are now being forced to meet it by devising measures of a more permanent character.

Controlling Investment

I pass to the second main field of control. Free investment was regarded as the undisputed right of the entrepreneur under the old regime and is still so regarded as his right over a considerable field of enterprise. I have deliberately refrained from dealing with problems associated with economic fluctuations, which are also problems directly related to the flow of investment. But assuming that periodic economic fluctuations are eliminated, there is still an unsolved problem of investment. Progress means continuous investment in new enterprises. It means the devising of new methods, the production of new commodities, the provision of new services for consumers. All this requires the expansion of investment into new fields. Is there any guarantee that this will take place automatically under free enterprise? Is there any reason to suppose that old industries will not be grossly over-capitalized or that they will be organized on the most efficient plan? I think not. In Australia the tariff board in its survey of protected industries has revealed very disturbing examples of over-capitalized industries —boots and shoes, textiles, cement. We have recently had a survey of the flour and bread industries by a royal commission. This survey shows how costly unrestricted private enterprise is in these two industries. Inefficiency in these industries and over-capitalization in other industries would be avoided or greatly reduced by some collective effort to provide information, and to eliminate overlapping of effort and plant. The industries themselves apparently will not make the effort on their own account. It will be necessary for the state sooner or later to insist upon the effort's being made. But it will be necessary to avoid action that will preserve old technique because of the fear of over-capitalization. The right of the entrepreneur to duplicate plant and equipment in an industry already fully capitalized will doubtless be denied the entrepreneur in the future, unless he satisfies a constituted authority that he can make a real contribution to the efficiency of the industry. This development will be resisted because the entrepreneur is impatient of any restriction upon his freedom. He has to be reminded of the words of a great Harvard philosopher:

'A great society is a society in which its men of business think greatly of their functions.' If saving is a virtue, investment becomes the cardinal economic achievement. Society has everything to gain by increasing its stock of capital and improving its social equipment. To suggest that the motive of private profit is the best guide and inspiration to this development is childish folly. We want to maintain the driving force of the profit motive, but to avoid the wastes and errors of competitive investment.

Collective Goods and Services

Lastly we come to the role of the state in providing, or ensuring the provision of, an increasing flow of goods and services that will not normally be provided by private enterprise. This is partly a problem of investment and partly a problem of transforming increased technical efficiency into a higher standard of living. Without this action by the state the world will be denied some of the best fruits of the application of science to industry. Political economy was nurtured in the cradle of physiocratic doctrine, which taught that wealth came directly from the soil, and made a foolish but far-reaching distinction between productive and unproductive labor. Economics has not yet emancipated itself fully from this doctrine, which has also cast its spell over the entrepreneur and is a firmly rooted belief of the primary producer, who has a greater influence on political policy than he thinks. It is at the root of the popular complaints against so-called rural depopulation. It is responsible more than anything else for the survival of a Calvinistic fear that the world is deteriorating because it enjoys the fruits of its labors. Yet a moment's reflection will show how great has been the progress, in all countries that enjoy a high standard of living, of the provision of what I have called collective goods and services—education, public health services, libraries, parks and playing grounds, roads, municipal and government buildings, museums and picture galleries, better housing of the poor, broadcasting. This is state control of consumption. Without state action these services would have been provided for a few who could afford them. The world would have been poorer. As the economic system, exploiting the resources of science, yields its fruit more abundantly, these services and goods will be provided in greater quantities. We are richer than we allow ourselves to think, and we could be richer still if we extended these services

even by reducing our consumption of the alluring but illusory products dangled before our eyes because they can be produced and sold at a profit. The services and goods I have in mind are what one of my colleagues has called 'tertiary' products, but they require some form of collective action for their production. They account in some measure for the increasing proportion of modern investment that is controlled by or directly made by the state. They take an increasing proportion of the productive effort of the community out of the hands of the entrepreneur. They involve the deliberate and compulsory transfer of part of the national income from private to public control.

I have said nothing of large-scale planning, which has become more important in every country. It necessarily must become so. We have it in the British Empire in migration and settlement. You in the United States have it in the Boulder Dam, the much disputed Tennessee Valley Authority, and the gigantic problems of shifting soil and erosion in the prairies. England has it in the grid system in electricity and in transport. These are problems that can only be faced by concerted community effort. Their solution is quite impossible by the entrepreneur alone. They involve long-range effort in which the scope for error is very great; and many errors are made. These errors are quoted again and again as an example of the inevitable inefficiency of state enterprise, when for the most part they are the results of political interference in the conception and administration of the enterprise. I have discussed this point already, but it must be repeated that the state will be compelled to devise a system of planning independent of the politician, whose business it is to debate large problems of policy after hearing expert opinion and attempting to reconcile it with lay opinion. This can be done best by the commission or board, working subject to general policy laid down by Parliament, but possessing initiative in planning and independence in management. It is only fair to the advocate of state enterprise to insist that the state gets the difficult jobs—those in which the planning must be at very long range and the margin of profit, if any, small. The entrepreneur, like the pirate tramp ship and the motor carrier, skims the cream of the trade and leaves the rest to the state. It is thus all the more important that the state should take extreme care in providing itself with expert administrators.

The Future of the Entrepreneur

There is ample evidence in the trend of social policy in many countries to support the main conclusions of this paper. The state is assuming more and more the functions of the entrepreneur or exercising more and more control over the entrepreneur. This I believe to be the inevitable result of the rise of capitalism, with its enlarged scale of operations, increased complexity of organization, and greater productivity. There is a fundamental change in the attitude of the entrepreneur; more and more enlightened entrepreneurs preach the gospel of the social responsibility of their class. But it cannot be left to the class as a whole to discharge these responsibilities without state intervention; nor can it be left to the entrepreneur class to supply all the goods and services of modern industry and undertake all the long-range planning of modern communities. The transformation to controlled economy and the state as entrepreneur in many fields of enterprise has gone far in most countries. There is a danger that it may go too far, as perhaps it has under dictatorships. In the English-speaking world democracy still prevails; its continuance depends in no small part upon the future of the entrepreneur. We in Australia have inherited some of the British capacity for compromise. We are not logical, but we can improvise a solution of a problem when we have to face one. In 1931 we acted on the impulse of fair treatment to all, and we invoked the power of the state to enforce it. But having provided a basis upon which to reconstruct our impaired fortunes, through a liberal banking policy and public works expenditure, we encouraged the entrepreneur to make his own effort to recovery unimpeded by restrictive state action. Much the same comment is true of Britain, the other British dominions, and the Scandinavian democracies. Here we have what I think is the sound conception of the relation of the state to the entrepreneur. You aim at getting the best of both possible worlds, and you succeed if your entrepreneur recognizes the justice and sound economic sense of some degree of control, while your democracy recognizes on its part that the entrepreneur should be encouraged to make his great contribution to economic and social progress. In this way we reconcile authority and the individual—the combination of control, where that is necessary, with the exercise of initiative and responsibility by the individual in his own sphere.

I am not extolling the virtues of the British system, but merely drawing attention to a trend of industrial evolution which I think will exercise great influence upon our central problem. It is your greatest problem in the United States, and your future democratic system will in large measure depend upon its solution. If the people come to distrust the entrepreneur he will after years of bitter conflict be eliminated. If the entrepreneur kicks against the pricks he may maintain a privileged position, and eventually impose some authoritarian system upon the country. Neither solution appeals to me, if I may be permitted to say so, as rational for the United States, or in keeping with the democratic tradition of the country. You must build a bridge between them so that you will allow your native genius for rapid development under individual enterprise to flourish. After the state has entered fully into its new sphere as entrepreneur or as an agency for control, there will still remain wide scope for the exercise by the entrepreneur of those gifts of imagination, courage, and initiative which have done more than anything else to build up your industrial system. But the gifts will at last yield their full fruits because they will not be offset by the entrepreneur's neglect of his high social function.

In this hall of learning in the oldest university in the United States I have been all too conscious of my limitations to deal with a central problem in economics, and one that is daily engaging the attention of many respected economists in this and other great American universities. My only claim to speak is that I come from a country which knows the failures and the successes of state enterprise. I belong to a small band of economists who have had the opportunity of participating in discussions upon the formulation of economic policy and the devising of appropriate administrative machinery. Our problems are simple, compared with yours, and we are able perhaps to measure our economic forces with a little more precision, and to educate our masters a little more effectively. But I have no wish to draw from our limited experience conclusions of wide application. We, in common with other British countries, have problems enough yet to solve, and I am happy to be among my fellow economists in the United States once more to learn from them what lessons your own experience has to offer in developing forms of economic control that will improve the efficiency of the entrepreneur and reconcile his interests with those of the state.